extraordinary parenting

Eloise Rickman is a parent educator who works with clients around the world through online courses and coaching, and through her Instagram account @mightymother_. Her work focuses on evidence-based parenting, home education, and helping families find more rhythm and ease in their daily lives. She is a trained doula, and previously studied social anthropology at Cambridge University, where she first became interested in how childhood and family practices shape society. She lives in south London with her husband, Sam, and young daughter, Frida, who has been home educated from birth.

extraordinary parenting

the essential guide
to parenting and
educating at home

Eloise Rickman

SCRIBE
Melbourne • London

Scribe Publications
2 John St, Clerkenwell, London, WC1N 2ES, United Kingdom
18–20 Edward St, Brunswick, Victoria 3056, Australia
3754 Pleasant Ave, Suite 100, Minneapolis, Minnesota 55409 USA

Published by Scribe in 2020

Typeset in Adobe Garamond by J&M Typesetting

Printed and bound in the UK by CPI Group (UK) Ltd, Croydon CR0 4YY

Scribe Publications is committed to the sustainable use of natural resources
and the use of paper products made responsibly from those resources.

9781913348540 (UK edition)
9781922310460 (Australian edition)
9781950354504 (US edition)
9781925938647 (ebook)

Catalogue records for this book are available from the National Library of
Australia and the British Library.

scribepublications.co.uk
scribepublications.com.au
scribepublications.com

For Frida.
My bones will always love your bones.

Contents

Contents

Contents

Contents

Preface

As I write this, for the first time in history, schools and childcare settings in countries across the world have been closed to the majority of children, with no set date to reopen; everyone has been instructed to stay home due to the COVID-19 virus.

This is a worrying time for families, who find themselves juggling childcare and working from home, alongside reduced income and job losses, and the anxiety and health concerns that come with a global pandemic. Millions of parents have suddenly found themselves in the position of effectively having to home educate their children, without any of the resources or research that families who ordinarily homeschool would have access to. And even families who usually home-school are finding themselves doing so without the groups, classes, museums, parks, and public libraries that form a part of their daily lives.

As a peaceful-parenting and home-education coach who has worked with parents all over the world, in recent weeks my inbox has been filled with messages from worried parents looking for support, advice, and ideas as they face unprecedented circumstances. Although the internet is full of well-meaning suggestions, the endless resources out there can feel overwhelming. So I asked myself what *I* wanted to help me get through this difficult time, and the answer was — as the answer always is when I ask myself what I want — a book.

And so — quickly, urgently — this book was born. Drawing on the many resources I've created over the years for use with my clients, it is a practical, evidence-based guide to calmly parenting and educating from home as you navigate uncertain times, and to building strong, flexible rhythms that will see your family through both the good days and the more challenging ones. Although I wrote this book with the COVID-19 crisis at the front of my mind — how could I not have done? — my hope is that it will guide you through parenting and educating more intentionally, bringing calm and connection to your home, whichever season of your life you find yourself in.

Introduction

We are living through extraordinary times.

When unexpected things happen, it is difficult and worrying, and it's easy for us to feel powerless. But the good news is that we aren't. We may not be able to cure global diseases or halt climate change in its tracks, but we do have one incredibly powerful tool at our disposal with which we can change the world: our parenting.

Parenting can be a truly radical act. The way in which we raise our children can have a profound positive (or negative) impact on our families, our communities, and our world.

When things are tough, focusing on how we parent can take a back seat as we try to keep everyone safe, fed, and relatively happy, while dealing with our own fears. But although times of crisis can challenge us, testing our resilience to its limits, they also offer a unique opportunity for us as parents to re-evaluate what is important to us and to deeply reconnect with our children.

That's what this book is about: helping your family to thrive amid the uncertainty of modern life. Because, no matter what else is happening, one thing is for sure: your children need you right now.

The five pillars of parenting and educating at home

Even during moments of crisis, there are some simple steps that you can take to keep your family feeling calm and connected to one another, creating a raft of safety and stability to carry your children through the roughest of seas.

These five steps form the core of raising and educating children, and they are relevant no matter how old your children and no matter what is going on around you:

1 Prioritising family relationships; deepening your connection to your children through playful and empathic parenting.

2 Building strong, adaptable rhythms to provide your children with predictability and security, even when the world feels uncertain and strange.

3 Creating a calm, simplified home environment that will encourage deep play and independence, a haven in which you can shelter in tough times.

4 Exploring enjoyable ways of learning together as a family; finding ways to help your children thrive while exploring their own unique interests and abilities.

5 Taking care of your own needs as a parent, allowing you to be the parent your children need.

I want to be clear that this book is not a curriculum; it doesn't contain a detailed set of exercises to work through with your child at home, or a step-by-step method for teaching them to read or write. Instead, it offers the building blocks to help you create a home atmosphere in which natural, joyful learning will flourish. Whether you choose to take a more informal, child-led approach to education, or you prefer to work from textbooks and worksheets, the foundation of rich, happy home-based learning is the same.

The first three chapters of *Extraordinary Parenting* will aid you in building this foundation. Chapter One will help you nurture a secure, joyful relationship with your child; Chapter Two will teach you how to craft a strong family rhythm; and Chapter Three will guide you through preparing your home environment to meet your child's needs, foster independence, and encourage independent play. In Chapter Four, you'll find practical tips and ideas for educating your child at home, whatever their age and whether you've always planned to homeschool or been plunged into it unexpectedly. Finally, Chapter Five will help you to make space for your own needs as a parent, because, when it comes to parenting and homeschooling, *you* are your child's most precious resource. Dotted through the book are snippets from conversations I've had with parents and experts, as well as mentions of studies and books that I've found eye-opening and illuminating. You'll find links to all of these, as well as a small selection of my favourite homeschooling books and websites, at the end of the book.

As well as a curriculum, the other thing you won't find in this book are instructions to buy piles of new materials or toys, or pay for expensive courses or resources. You likely already have many of the most important things you need to set up a successful environment for educating your child at home: some great books, some kitchen ingredients, a few toys, and a loving parent. (In fact, you may find yourself getting rid of things, as you realise that, when it comes to physical stuff, less is so much more for children.) Likewise, you don't need a big house or a garden to give your child an amazing childhood and education — all the suggestions in this book will work whatever the size of your home. Nor do you need to have hours of free time at your disposal every day. I juggle homeschooling my daughter with a busy work schedule, so I get it — your time is a precious commodity. Many of the ideas I suggest can be implemented in a short space of time, and even the bigger projects — such as crafting a family rhythm, or toy rotation — can be done in an evening, and will free up more time than they take you.

Educating at home

I know that both parenting and home educating can feel daunting; after all, our children only get one childhood, and we want to make it wonderful. But you are the best possible parent for your child — and the best equipped person to help them learn. No matter how fantastic teachers are, they will never know or love your child as much as you do. You and your child are a team.

If your children are out of school unexpectedly, whether due to illness, family issues, or an unexpected crisis, it is understandable that you might be worrying about what they are missing out on. A mother I know whose three school-age children are home due to COVID-19 confessed that she felt enormous anxiety about her ability to educate her children:

'I keep looking at the pile of worksheets they are meant to be doing and worrying that I can't possibly keep up. I feel devastated about what they are missing out on; they cry about missing their friends, and I feel like they're just bored.' If you are not homeschooling through choice, but by necessity, you may relate to these feelings — especially if you've never contemplated home-based education before.

But unplanned home education isn't always unwelcome. I've spoken to many parents who have told me that they've been grateful for the opportunity to have more time with their children, to give them an extra slice of childhood, free from homework and uniform, and to road-test what home education might look like for their families long-term.

In this book, you'll learn how to ignite your child's wonder and curiosity, and tap into their inner motivation to learn. You'll discover how to go beyond drilling your child on the 'three Rs' as you start to see how the lessons you give them don't need to be defined by a formal curriculum, but instead can be inspired by the everyday events and discoveries that form the fabric of your life together: a leaf found in the street leading to learning about the seasons, a TV show prompting a project on sharks.

I know from my conversations with parents that many families are walking the tightrope between school and home-based education, with resources sent from teachers to complete at home, or future exams to prepare for. So, as well as exploring informal learning, we will also look at how you can approach formal learning resources, finding ways to make them really work for you and your child, and bringing them to life (without needing to learn advanced algebra or dust off your rusty German skills), rather than trying to replicate a traditional classroom experience at home.

As home educating families have long known, outside of the constraints of traditional schooling anything is possible. Educating at home can reduce the stress on your child, encourage their natural thirst for learning, and bring new interests to the fore. It can foster deep learning for the whole family as you are transported to the far reaches of the solar system, to ancient Egypt, or to the courts of Henry VIII. Far from being an inferior replacement for school, your home is already the best possible place for learning to happen.

My parenting philosophy: a beautiful childhood

In this book, I share ideas based on my experience both as a parent educator and as a busy home-educating parent. I hope that these ideas will change your life for the better in the same way that they've already changed mine.

They really have shaped my life, and not just since becoming a parent: I was home educated myself, for a short while. Those formative years — spent at the beach and the library, reading books and playing games, and spending long holidays with my grandparents — had an overwhelmingly positive impact on my childhood and identity well into adulthood. My mother was influenced by the Montessori approach, making me sandpaper letters and DIY materials, but my early years were mostly filled with play-based, child-led, natural education. My earliest memories are of dancing to my parents' music in the tiny flat we lived in, my father telling me stories which would have me crying with laughter, and my mother taking me to a local park every day, where I would visit the goldfish pond and lie in the long grass. My parents had little money, but my childhood was rich beyond belief. There was no distinction between learning and life; I learned because I was curious, and full of wonder, and alive. Learning was as natural to me as breathing.

I entered the UK's state-funded school system when I was six and a half, two years after my classmates, and stayed there until I went to Cambridge University to study social anthropology. It was at Cambridge that I first became interested in how childhood and family practices shape the societies we live in, and how, in turn, our culture shapes our view of children and childhood, and the way we raise and educate young people. Why do some cultures allow children to use knives from a young age when others put warning signs around playgrounds? Why do some parents share beds and meals and conversations with their children, while others opt for early nights and sleep training? Why are children given more autonomy — and respect — in some societies than in others? My eyes were opened; parenting no longer felt like something private, but rather something intensely political and powerful, with the potential for radical transformation. But it wasn't until I had my daughter, Frida, that this really hit home.

As a young adult, I didn't think too much about parenting and education after I left university. But when Frida was born, all of those questions started to resurface. What did it mean to raise a child who would be happy and kind? What should parenting for the kind of society I wanted to live in look like? Although I was due to return to my job as a government press officer after my maternity leave, I found myself thinking more and more about whether we could keep Frida at home. Whenever I talked to my husband about looking for childcare for her, I felt a little more heartbroken. The childhood I was gifted by my parents seemed cruelly out of reach for my own sweet baby, growing up far away from the beach and the slow, unhurried rhythms of my own infancy. Yet the more I devoured books on child development and learning, the more certain I felt that this simple, magical childhood, full of natural opportunities for learning and wonder, was something I craved for my daughter. After sleepless nights and heartfelt conversations, I took a deep breath, handed in my notice, and started reading everything I could find on home education.

I refer to this vision as 'a beautiful childhood': a childhood with strong family connections, laughter, play, and joyful learning, where children feel seen, heard, and valued for who they are. It's what I was given by my parents, it's what my husband and I work hard to give our daughter, and it's what I believe all children deserve. And the most beautiful thing about it? It's never too late to offer it.

What a beautiful childhood looks like will be different from one family to the next. It's not about home educating, throwing away the TV, or eating only organic food. Rather, it's about treating our children with respect and compassion, consciously slowing down and reclaiming our children's right to play, and creating a rhythmic, intentional home environment where our children feel safe and flourish. It is not about aiming for perfection, in parenting or in home-based education. It is about aiming for compassion — for ourselves, for our children, and for those around us — and about finding ways to weave this compassion into our everyday lives.

In times like these, more than ever, we will need to focus inwards on the relationships we are building with our children. We will need to remember that, more than any fact or topic, kindness and self-belief are the most important things we can teach them. We will need to dig deep to find reserves of strength and patience we didn't realise we had, as we reassure our children that the world is a safe place (even as we worry that it is not). We will need to take deep breaths, apologise, and learn how to be with each other — present, human, imperfect — whatever life throws at us.

Many of the suggestions I share with you have their roots in the Montessori and Waldorf philosophies, as well as the Nonviolent Communication approach and my experience as a peaceful-parenting coach and home-educator. But even without these ideas, I want you to know that you are already good enough. You don't need to be an expert, or a teacher. You just need to be a parent. You know your children better than anyone, and you love them more than anyone. You are enough.

These are extraordinary times, and they call for extraordinary parenting. But I know you're up to the challenge.

Chapter One

Calm in the storm

When times are tough, it can be tempting to focus on the tangible: to buy more stuff, or make colourful charts and detailed plans. I get it — that's my first reaction too. But if we take a step back, the most valuable thing we can do as parents at any time — but especially during periods of uncertainty — is to focus on building a strong, positive relationship with our children where they feel heard, safe, and loved. This is especially important when spending more time together under the same roof; more time together means more opportunities for conflict and frustration — for kids and for parents — especially when you add change, stress, and worry into the mix. But the good news is that these opportunities for conflict — sibling arguments, tantrums, fights over tooth brushing — also offer us an opportunity each time to connect and deepen our relationships with our children.

This is far harder than ordering a heap of new toys or pulling out pens and paper to make a fancy schedule. But putting your relationship with your children first is what will allow them to thrive. In this chapter, we're going to look at some ideas that will help you to nurture these relationships and guide your child through daily life, whatever comes your way.

Nurturing growing brains

A positive parent–child relationship is vital for children's health, happiness, and resilience well into adulthood. Human emotional development is based on how we were treated early on in our lives; the way we were raised has a direct impact on our brain's development, with the first few years of our lives being the most critical. Varied research in neuroscience tells us that children's experiences quite literally shape their brains: each experience strengthens new pathways in the brain (neural pathways), which in turn shape our children's behaviours and world-view. These early childhood experiences also go on to shape future brain development, with researchers finding that mental stimulation from parents at the age of four was the key factor in predicting the development of several parts of the brain 15 years later (Avants et al., 2015). We know that children's brains are highly malleable, or 'plastic', and that they will change and adapt to their experiences and environments. This plasticity continues into adulthood — this is why when we practise something enough, we can do it without really thinking — but it is strongest in childhood. The early years of childhood matter.

Attachment theory, a term coined by John Bowlby in the 1950s, tells us that we are social animals who come into the world programmed to form attachments with other people. When caregivers respond positively to their baby's needs and behaviours — comforting them when they cry, holding and cuddling them, feeding them when they are hungry, cooing at their smiles — they lay the basis for a strong attachment, which in turn provides a secure base for exploring the world around them. Joyful, loving interactions and secure attachment are vital building blocks for self-worth, healthy social and physical development, and emotional intelligence. As Robin Grille writes in *Parenting for a Peaceful World*, 'Each parental smile and affectionate look "actually helps the brain to grow".'

It makes sense that when children's physical and emotional needs are responded to and met repeatedly, and they are treated with love, kindness, compassion, and warmth, they are likely to develop an expectation of a supportive world. We don't need studies to tell us that if a child experiences consistent emotional support and care, they are more likely to be inclined towards friendly, kind, and considerate behaviour; as parents, we have seen that our children are like little sponges, soaking up our words, behaviour, and mannerisms (most parents will recognise the horror of having our bad language or habits reflected back at us by our sweet children!).

Reading that the first few years of life are so influential to child development can be upsetting for some parents. I've had clients who struggled with post-natal depression, physical health issues, back-to-back pregnancies, and other difficulties that made it difficult for them to meet their child's needs in the early years. I want to say to you what I have said to them: *It is never too late to start building a loving, close, attached relationship with your child.* The best time to start is now.

Here are some things you can do to foster a secure attachment with your child:

- Show physical and verbal affection. Give them your undivided attention and presence for some time each day.
- Truly listen to them when they speak, taking them seriously.
- Treat them as equals, albeit ones who have less life experience and are still learning some skills. Respect their opinions and knowledge.
- Give them the freedom to try new things, with the space to fail and make mistakes. Give them responsibility that is appropriate to their age and skill.
- Support their choices; don't say no too often.
- Speak kindly about them to others, especially when they are in earshot.
- Create an environment where they can succeed and be independent; help your child when they ask you to, don't if they don't.

Building resilience

One aspect of children's development which is well supported by a positive parent–child relationship is resilience. There is no universal definition of resilience, but generally it is thought of as the ability to cope well with difficulty or stress. Resilience is associated with self-confidence, autonomy, emotional intelligence, and social competence.

With mental health issues in young children on the rise (in the UK, at least one in ten children between five and 16 have a diagnosed mental health disorder, with 8,000 under-tens diagnosed with depression), resilience is a topic of increasing interest. There is a growing body of evidence which suggests that children's ability to cope — or not — with the everyday challenges of childhood is a good predictor for the subsequent development of stress-related illnesses such as anxiety and depression.

As parents, we want our children to be resilient, to cope well with stress and change. We can support this by being attuned to their needs and supporting them lovingly, but also by recognising when they may benefit from opportunities to develop greater independence.

Here are some strategies to help your child develop resilience:

Avoid labels.

Labelling children as smart, naughty, clever, sensitive, lazy, messy, grumpy, etc. can make them start to believe those statements are true. Even if the words you use are positive — i.e. 'clever' — they can actually hinder growth, as the child feels their character is fixed. As a parent, you might consider saying, 'I can see that you worked really hard at this picture,' rather than, 'You're a natural artist.'

Help them learn to reframe.

Encourage your child to switch their focus from what they can't do to what they can do, or help them to see a situation from a different angle to focus less on negative outcomes. Your child might be frustrated that it's raining outside, but perhaps this is a good opportunity to build a rain gauge out of a plastic bottle or pull on wellies to go and look for snails.

Coach them through challenging situations ...

If they are having a tough time, don't ignore their reality and tell them everything is fine; instead, gently guide them to take a more nuanced view, asking them questions about how they might be able to face the problem themselves or how they would like your support.

... But let them work problems out on their own.

This can start early in life, by giving even very young children the space and trust to try moving through conflict to a resolution themselves; for example, watching from a close distance without getting involved as your young child gets into an argument at the playground, or giving siblings some room to work out disagreements by themselves. We are often quick to jump in and solve our children's problems for them — I can certainly empathise with this urge — but having the chance to try to fix problems and get it wrong sometimes is key if children are to develop resilience.

Appreciate their need to experience disappointment,
challenge, failure, and stress.

Children need these opportunities to develop the skills that will help them to live well in society. As a parent, you cannot shield your child from all pain and hurt, but you can provide a non-judgemental space for your child's emotions and mistakes. Almost all parents find it difficult to see their child upset — it's normal for our children's sadness to feel almost physically painful for us

— but sometimes our attempts to prevent our children's disappointment or frustration are less about meeting their needs and more about our own discomfort or fears. By distracting our children from sadness, we send the implicit message that sadness (or disappointment, or anger) is not okay.

Encourage them to reflect positively on their own ability to cope.

If your child has gone through a challenge, recognise their ability to cope during the experience, and reflect it back to them. Talk about them positively. For example, 'You felt really nervous. But you did it,' or 'It was hard when Nanna died — we all felt sad, and we still feel sad now when we miss her. But we also feel happy when we think about her, don't we?'

Take a balanced attitude to risk-taking and childhood independence.

Many children now are discouraged from taking even small risks, and not given much independence at all; this is something I often witness in playgrounds or at the park, with children chided for getting mud on their hands or for climbing 'too high' up a climbing frame. The amount of risk children can be safely exposed to will, of course, vary, depending on age and ability — I'm not suggesting you let your young child cross the road by themselves, or allow your thirteen-year-old to go backpacking alone — but there are many benefits to risky play that allows children to assess danger for themselves, something they will need to learn to do eventually.

As parents, we cannot build resilience in our children overnight. But consistently showing up with love and empathy, even when they are having a hard time, is the vital first step in helping them to thrive, no matter what is going on around us. One of the things that can help us do this as parents is understanding that our children's challenging behaviour isn't evidence that they are naughty or trying to upset us, but a sign that they need our help.

Understanding behaviour as a form of communication

Challenging behaviour, such as pushing, throwing, hitting, and being rude and defiant, will be familiar to all parents. When our children act in these ways, it can be draining and frustrating — and it can make us seriously question our parenting skills. The thing that has most transformed my parenting — and my ability to not completely lose it if my daughter draws on the wall or refuses to put her pyjamas on — is to remember that children's challenging behaviour is *always* a form of communication.

An oft-used metaphor is that of an iceberg. Visible to us is our child's behaviour, but underneath the waves might be hiding:

- Hunger or thirst

- Tiredness
- Physical discomfort (too hot, too cold, itchy clothes, over-stimulated, too much background noise)
- Feeling unwell or in pain
- Feeling upset
- Feeling lonely, or disconnected from parents or caregivers
- Feeling overwhelmed
- A need for sensory input or stimulation
- Feeling frustrated or angry
- Curiosity or experimentation
- A lack of self-control
- Issues at childcare or school
- Issues with another adult or child
- Changes in their life (new home, new sibling, divorce)
- Changes in the world around them
- Changes in their routine or rhythm
- Not being able to communicate or express themselves fully
- Not understanding why they cannot do something
- The reaction they received last time they behaved this way

In short, when children behave in a way that challenges us, they do so because they either need our help, our support, our guidance, or all three. They are not *giving us* a hard time, they are *having* a hard time! No one wants to be out of control, hurt people, or say things that are upsetting to hear. Children are always doing their best. By turning to punishment ('Get to your room!'), distraction ('Stop crying, look, here's a cookie') or shaming ('Why can't you just be good like your sister?') in these moments, we miss out on a precious opportunity for connection and building our relationship.

A classic example would be our child doing something they know they're not supposed to do, such as drawing on the wall, to meet their need for connection with us because they know that this will get our attention. In this situation, we could either punish the child, causing them (further) suffering by denying them the connection they are seeking and inflicting punishments on top of that. Or we can put our relationship with our child first, and respond with empathy and kindness to their attempt to reach out to us, reconnecting with them and showing them that we love them unconditionally and will help them when they need us.

I want to be clear that I am not advocating for permissive parenting, where there are no rules or limits. Setting limits is important for everyone's happiness. In our family, the limits are relatively simple: 1. Hurt no one, including emotional harm and physical harm (this would cover, for example, brushing teeth, as not doing so would eventually cause physical harm, as well as the more obvious scenarios); and 2. Damage no thing. Anything outside of this can be discussed and negotiated. In the second scenario above, where we respond to our child's behaviour empathically, we can still make it clear that certain things — in this case, drawing on the wall — are unacceptable and not permitted. But we can do so kindly, while imagining how our child is feeling in this moment and always trusting that they are doing the best that they can.

This shift requires a radical move away from parenting that is based on discipline and punishment as the core mechanisms to *change* our children's behaviour. Instead, here we are seeking to *understand* what needs are underlying their behaviour, and seeking to meet those needs. When we are having a hard time as adults, this is what we would want from the people we love. Our children are no different.

When we start to view behaviour as a form of communication — when we see hitting another child not as an act of malice, but rather our child telling us, 'I need your help right now' — then it is much easier to respond peacefully and calmly, and with the empathy that our children deserve. Although it can be so frustrating when our children act in ways which are difficult for us — especially when we are struggling too — we should remember that they are still learning self-control and finding ways to express themselves. We can help them by responding to their behaviour with empathy, and giving them the benefit of the doubt.

Sometimes behaviour which we might think of as 'naughty' is simply our child exploring the world around them, or finding a way to get their needs met creatively. I remember when my daughter was a toddler watching her very deliberately fetch a glass of water from the kitchen sink, carry it over to the dining room, and pour it on the floor. I was so taken aback by her purposeful behaviour that, rather than stepping in, I just watched her. She immediately walked off only to come back with her little mop, and quickly, quietly, she began mopping the wooden floor. I was so stunned; had I stepped in to tell her off, not only would I have created unnecessary conflict, but I would have missed this amazing moment of self-directed work. Worse, I would have shown her that my assumption was that she was acting from a place of mischief rather than of helpfulness.

I'm sure there have been many moments like this that I have missed, where I have stepped in too soon, but it was a powerful reminder to trust her intentions. It can help to remember that you're on the same team as your child; that they don't want to create more work or stress for you, and that you want to parent as well as you can, but that inevitably you will both fail at times because you are only human. When you start approaching things as a team, a lot of conflict disappears. Rather than parenting from the top down, when an issue arises, you can talk to your child. Ask them what would help them stick to the limit you have in place, talk to them about their needs, and look for solutions together. If your child breaks a glass by throwing it on the ground, you could punish them by confiscating a toy, or shout at them, or shame them by saying, 'Why are you acting like a baby?' Or you could give them the benefit of the doubt and ask them, 'Why did you throw the glass?' You can then involve them in thinking through what could be done about it, how it could be cleaned safely, and what would happen if someone stepped on the floor now, explaining that broken glass can be dangerous. You can of course still reiterate that glasses are not meant for throwing, but either they didn't know this, in which case punishment and shaming is unfair, or they did know, in which case there is likely something going on under the tip of the iceberg which means that punishment would make it even harder to meet their needs.

This is just as important for older children and teenagers,

too. If your teen stays out later than expected, rather than pouncing on them the moment they step through the door, think about what your goal is. Is it blind obedience, or a deeper, more trusting relationship? Ask them why they stayed out late, discuss your own worries, and make a plan for what they could do next time they find themselves out later than expected. Perhaps you'll find yourself reminiscing about your own broken curfews! This kind of parenting is not easy at first, especially if it's not how you were raised, but gradually your child will learn that you're on their side and want to work together.

When you start to view challenging behaviour not as naughtiness which needs training, punishing, or discipline, but as a problem to solve together, the dynamic of your parenting shifts and conflicts can become opportunities for connection.

It is when children are at their most challenged — and challenging — that they most need our reassurance, and unconditional love. And although responding in this way takes practice, the effect it has on the whole family will be well worth it.

When you disagree on parenting styles

It's not uncommon for my clients to have very different parenting styles to their co-parents, with one parent typically more in favour of traditional disciplinary methods, such as time-outs and punishments. This can understandably cause a lot of conflict and worry for parents who don't agree with these methods. Some minor inconsistency in parenting styles is inevitable, and probably healthy and flexible. But if your child is hearing wildly different messages around what they are allowed and not allowed to do then it will make it challenging for them to understand what is expected of them, and can put strain on familial relationships.

If you're finding yourself locking horns with your co-parent, my advice would be to go back to the basics together. What do you want for your child? What kind of relationship do you hope to have with them? What words would you like your child to use to describe you when they are grown? Re-establishing some common ground between you and remembering that you both have similar goals — even if you have different methods of getting there — can help bring you together, even as you have challenging discussions. Using some of the positive communication tips I suggest in this chapter will help too; you both need to accept that you are doing your best, so you can solve any problems that arise together.

Unconditional Positive Regard

One of the most important gifts we can give our children is that of Unconditional Positive Regard. Coined by the psychologist Carl Rogers, it means that, when we're interacting with someone, we choose to accept and think the best of them, regardless of what they say or do. A powerful therapeutic tool, this is also valuable for the parent–child relationship.

When we see our children as inherently good, and their behaviour as simply them doing their best to get their needs met in whatever way they know how, then we allow them to develop a strong, positive sense of self-worth.

When we adopt an unconditionally positive attitude towards our children — parenting them without trying to change them — we allow them the freedom and emotional safety to try new things, make mistakes, and take risks. We show them that, whatever they do, they are loved, important, and good.

This doesn't mean they will never get things wrong — far from it, many of their choices may end up having negative consequences. But when we allow ourselves to see the good in our children on even the toughest of days, we set the basis for calm, loving communication.

So how does this look in practice? What happens if your child does something 'wrong', such as hitting their sibling?

- Focus on their feelings, rather than behaviour: 'I can see you're feeling really angry that he took your toy.'
- Gently stop them from repeating the action: 'I'm just going to hold your hand until you feel you can stop hitting, because I need to keep your brother safe.'
- Not withdrawing love. Children who are at their most difficult to love are in a place where they need our love, comfort, hugs, and reassurance more than ever: 'I love you so much. I can see you're feeling frustrated, but I will not let you hit him again.'

As parents, the most powerful thing we can do is to model the sort of behaviour we want to see, showing up as the kind of humans we would like our children to grow into. This is much more difficult than meting out punishments or shouting: it requires us to work hard on ourselves first. It means we need to practise what we preach, to exercise self-control, to be vulnerable and authentic. But it is the most important thing we can do, and our best bet if we want to protect our relationship with our children while giving them a chance to develop a strong sense of autonomy and self-worth.

This kind of parenting can feel so challenging at times, especially if you were raised without this kind of Unconditional Positive Regard. But keep repeating to yourself: *My child's worth is non-negotiable, whatever they do.* And by the way, the same goes for you too.

Moving away from control-based parenting

When things feel uncertain, we often seek to control the things we can. Children are no different; it's why, when they feel stressed, children may restrict the foods they eat, refuse to go to bed, start wetting themselves when they've been dry for months, or act in a seemingly aggressive or destructive way. Through this behaviour, they are simply exerting control over the few things they have power over.

You have the opportunity to hand over to your children genuine control and choice over many areas of their lives, reducing stress and conflict for the whole family. Here are some things you may want to take a look at giving your children more autonomy over:

- How much they eat at meal times, trusting them when they say they are full or if they are still hungry.

- What clothes they wear, including whether or not they wear a coat in cooler weather.
- Hugs, kisses, and physical contact. It's never too early to build a culture of consent in your home.
- How they play (perhaps using toys in ways they were not intended to be used).

The more autonomy you can grant your children, the happier your family will be.

Keeping calm in a crisis

How we communicate with our children matters even more during times of uncertainty. Imagine yourself on a plane, experiencing heavy turbulence. How the pilot and the cabin crew act will have a big impact on your feelings, and how you in turn react to the situation. If the crew sound panicked, anxious, or irritated, it will likely increase your own feelings of worry. Dismissing the problem and telling you there's nothing to worry about may also increase your levels of stress; you can tell something isn't right, so why aren't they being honest about it? If, on the other hand, the crew sound calm, honest, and in control — 'The turbulence is a little heavier than usual but it's still normal. We hope to come out of it soon and we will keep you updated; in the meantime, let us know if you have any questions or need anything' — you may find yourself able to relax a little more. The situation is not ideal, but you feel safe in their capable hands, and you're pleased to know your concerns aren't being dismissed. You trust them to get you through.

As you navigate your own turbulence as a family, your children will look to your leadership to steer them through. How you respond to these events, and how you communicate with your children during times of illness, crisis, or change, can have a big impact on how they will feel and respond to what's happening around them.

Talking to children about uncertainty

As TV host Mr Rogers famously said, 'When I was a boy and I would see scary things in the news, my mother would say to me, "Look for the helpers. You will always find people who are helping."' This can be a helpful way to approach unavoidable conversations around crises with young children, focusing on the positive ways people are working to help others.

Talking to children about difficult or uncertain situations needs to be done in a way which is calm and age appropriate, helps them feel safe, and explains the changes to routine or daily life your child may be experiencing. A good rule of thumb is to tell them what they need to know, and no more. With young children in particular, it is important to keep conversations factual, short, and as positive as possible while being honest. Adding to children's fears won't benefit anyone.

If the change or uncertainty you are facing will have a direct impact on your family and those around you, share a simple plan with your children on how you will be navigating this ('Grandma is not very well at the moment, so let's draw her some lovely pictures and then I can take them over to her later to cheer her up'). Be willing to answer any questions your children have honestly but sensitively ('Is Grandma going to die?' 'The doctors are working very hard to make her better, and I hope she will live a long time. But right now we don't know if she will get better'). Brainstorm ideas as a family of kind and helpful things you can do.

If the situation is bigger than your immediate family — affecting your community, country, or the world — and your children are in childcare or in school, then you might want to ask them what they've heard about the situation, and if they have any questions about anything they've heard. At home, you may prefer to keep radio and television news off entirely around younger children, and to limit it around teens — research shows that negative TV news can have a detrimental impact on mental health (Johnston & Davey, 1997). For similar reasons, if possible, try to keep adult conversations about worries for when the children are in bed.

Supporting children through change

I spoke to Carine Robin, an experienced psychologist and Montessori teacher who has two school-age children herself, about how parents can support their children through uncertainty and changes. She said:

'Over the course of your children's lives, it's almost certain that as a family you will face some challenges: divorce, illnesses, death of a grandparent, job loss, or financial burden. Life is full of uncertainty.

'Going through a rough patch will impact your ability to parent. In fact, it has been proven that our ability to parent is directly correlated to our sense of safety. We need to feel safe and secure to cope with daily parenting challenges. It is similar for our children. They need to feel secure to be able to be emotionally balanced.

'Once faced with a difficult situation, it's essential that we, as parents, act like grown-ups. We have to try to keep our fears at bay and reassure our children, verbally and non-verbally, that we are going to be able to keep them safe and to get through the situation.

'I mainly work with parents of children under the age of six, and young children have a very immature brain; their neocortex is not fully developed. What that means is that a child of that age cannot reason like us. They don't project themselves in the future as we do. They also cannot distance themselves from the world's suffering. We could say that young children take everything personally. For example, if they hear on the news that someone has died, they will fear that you or they might die right now. Although it's okay to share the events we are going through with our children, it's also important to filter the adult world for them. You can express your feelings and share them with your children, but you don't have to explain all the little details of the situation.

'Children like facts and respond well to simple explanations, such as, "We wash our hands because that helps us not to get sick." There is no need to add any other reason, and there is no need for a panicked tone. It's obviously easier said than done. One way to help your children cope with any dramatic life event is to think about your own way of coping.

'The good news is that children are pretty resilient. What can help them as well is "playing it out". Children learn through play. They express themselves through play. In fact, in child therapy, we are mostly worried when children refuse to play. Use play to help your children to work through any traumatic situation. If your children are reluctant to talk about their fears and worries, grab two teddies and make them talk. If your child is recovering from surgery, buy her a doctor kit. Invite your child to draw his nightmare or what had happened at school. If you relax enough to join your child in their play, he will be more likely to listen to you and tell you how he feels after he has connected with you through play.'

Many of my clients have found that playful parenting techniques provide the perfect bridge back to connection and calm when their children are feeling overwhelmed or anxious. And play is proven to be an important tool for children to process their experiences and learn about the world.

Using play to support emotional development

Play is the way in which children make sense of the world and process experiences and emotions. As a parent, you will have seen that play is hardwired into children, wherever they are and whoever they are with. There is a huge wealth of research out there on the benefits of play for children young and old: academic, physical, emotional, and social. It's how they learn, how they develop; it's where they find flow, that magical state of being so absorbed in an activity of your choosing that you forget about everything else.

Our children's play is almost always more meaningful than it first appears. It can be a safe way for children to try out new skills and new ways of being, and it is a powerful way of healing from emotional distress, putting themselves in a position of power, and establishing closeness and connection. Play allows children to 'try out' different feelings, play-acting sadness or challenging experiences in a controlled way. When children are unable to release their emotions through play, they may instead release them through tantrums or challenging behaviours, such as hitting or pushing in frustration, or simply shutting down.

Making space and time to really play with our children is one of the greatest gifts we can give them, especially when navigating challenging times; it tells them that we have time for them, that they are our priority. When we get down on their level and enter into their world, whether it's building a block tower on the floor or asking them to show us how Minecraft works, playing by their rules, with them in charge, makes them feel safe and loved. This is even more important when things are changing in our child's life.

Playfulness can offer us a lifeline when it comes to reconnecting with our children during challenging moments, allowing us to constantly repair, rebuild, and strengthen our relationship with our children through daily life. Playful parenting is so much more than just getting down on the floor and 'playing'; it's an approach to everyday interactions with children which can help with the hardest parts of parenting — arguments, big emotions, anxiety — and bring more joy into every part of our life. It can help us to reconsider what it means to be a parent, and allow us to let go and tap into a more playful side of ourselves, not just in parenting but in our relationships and our work outside of the home, too.

Play is the perfect way to build up a strong relationship with our children. It is one of the best ways to keep our connection with our children 'topped up' and to repair and replenish it when it runs low. In his book *Playful Parenting*, Lawrence Cohen writes that, during times of disconnect, 'play can be the bridge back to that deep emotional bond between parent and child'. Often, reconnecting with our children puts an end to the challenging behaviour without any further redirection needed, because our child's need for connection has been met.

Challenging behaviour and playful parenting

As we saw earlier, challenging behaviour is almost always a cry for more love, more affirmation, more connection. It is a form of communication. And meeting that behaviour with play can be hugely powerful.

Although it can be really hard, catching yourself before you respond impatiently can make all the difference when your child is challenging you. I remember a moment when my daughter was a little younger, and she was trying to pull our cat's tail. I could have responded with frustration or disappointment, or bored us both with my lecturing: 'You know that you may never pull the cat's tail. Hands are for being gentle, not for hurting.' I might have succeeded in protecting the cat, but I'm not sure that I would have done anything for

Frida's need for connection. Thankfully, I was able to catch myself in time and respond playfully.

'FRIDA!' I said with overblown fake outrage, 'Did I just see you were about to try and grab the cat's tail? Well, maybe I will try to grab YOUR tail!' This was followed by a joyful period of roughhousing, chasing, and a lot of giggling and laughter. Connection was restored, conflict avoided, and joy injected into the situation. And best of all, the cat continued to snooze, blissfully unaware of the tail-pulling he had narrowly avoided, and we were all the happier for it.

Children don't misbehave because they are bad, or because they want to cause pain. They lash out because they are feeling pain themselves. De-escalating situations before they turn into full-blown conflicts, choosing connection and play to do so, is far more peaceful, powerful, easy, and effective — for everyone involved, including household pets! Sometimes we can't help ourselves, and we respond without thinking. But when we can take a moment to pause, breathe, and consider our response, choosing playful parenting can save the day.

Turning frowns upside down

Playfulness can also be a useful tool for us to help our children release their feelings and move on from moments of frustration or upset.

Recently, I was out with my daughter and she was in a terrible mood. I'd tried cuddles, empathic listening, distraction, reconnection, everything I could think of, but it wasn't shifting, and I knew that if it continued through lunch she'd end up not eating and then feeling worse than before. I had the sense that she was just as desperate as I was for her mood to shift, but she needed some help getting there.

Suddenly I had an idea. We were just leaving the park, so I said to her, 'You know, the grumpies you have all over you can't get past the gate and out of the park, so we're going to have to shake them all off before you can go into the cafe!' I asked her to stand in star pose, then shake and wiggle each part of her body in turn to shake them all away. 'Oh no! One of them is stuck in your hair!' I said, as I pretended to pick off an invisible creature. 'And one is on your arm!' Within a minute, she was happy and smiling, and we were able to carry on our day with a lot more joy than before. Some playfulness, some mindfulness, and some movement all came together to find the perfect cure for 'the grumpies'.

I have another game I sometimes play when my daughter is feeling cross and frustrated. She will say something like, 'I hate this supper.' Then I respond with fake outrage, saying, 'Yes, this supper is awful!' She will repeat what I say, 'This supper is awful!' Then I'll say, 'It is smelly and it's horrible! It's the worst supper in the world! This supper is absolutely disgusting!' all with a big frown on my face. We go on like this until we are both laughing, and the tension and annoyance has vanished. It's a much more effective response than me replying to 'I hate this supper' by saying, 'I know that's not true, you love this meal, come and sit down and eat it,' because it shows that I am listening to her, and allows me to help her with her feelings of frustration. A potentially fraught moment has been turned into an opportunity for connection.

Often the connection and laughter that playful parenting creates can come together to help shake off bad moods (for adults as well as children). When we get the timing right and our child is ready, play can be a great tool in bringing a child 'back' to us and helping them to move on from their bad mood so that they can enjoy the day. Often, once a child has been supported to fully express their feelings, they will seem happier and more relaxed than they had been previously.

Play helps children process

I spoke to Lisa Harmer, a dramatherapist and mother to two young children, about the power of play to help children make sense of the world around them. She said:

'Where we might use words to explore our experiences, children use story. Play is a language that they are fluent in. In this symbolic world, they are in control, they are safe, and they are able to communicate their needs and even have them met within their play.

'As parents, we can help by neutrally engaging with the play, and trusting our child will show us what they need us to know. It is not for us to control or fix, but rather bear witness to and acknowledge our child's feelings.'

Children are very rarely in a position of power in their daily lives. For the most part, they have little control over their schedule, what food they are offered, who looks after them, what they are expected to do, and how they are expected to behave.

Although simply being playful cannot change this fact,

play that puts children in a position of power can help them to overcome feelings of powerlessness, and support them to develop confidence and a sense of agency.

Four kinds of play are brilliant for helping children experiment with power relations, as well as letting them work through potentially upsetting or traumatic instances:

- Play where children are in charge. ('You be the child and I will be the teacher, and I'm going to give you lots of homework.')
- Play where children can re-enact and process difficult experiences. I have noticed that my daughter's doctor and vet play has increased dramatically since the start of the COVID-19 pandemic, which makes perfect sense; play is a safe place to explore scary thoughts like getting ill.
- Playful situations where children are allowed to be physically stronger. We often play games where our daughter can climb on us or physically 'get one over' on us, or otherwise outsmart or trick us.
- Play where children can experiment with pushing boundaries. We play a game called the topsy-turvy house where my daughter can say the opposite of what she is normally 'supposed' to say: 'I hate you! You are a terrible mummy!' This can be a wonderful, safe way of relieving tension.

Sal Gould, a teacher and the owner of children's mindfulness business Mindful Kin, agrees. She said:

'A great starting point for opening up conversations about children's emotions comes through observing their play.

Watch closely — do any themes emerge? Perhaps there is a new baby in the family and your child is acting out a scenario where the baby goes back to the hospital and life resumes as before. You can begin to put a label on these feelings. For example, "Jade is feeling jealous because Mummy is spending lots of time feeding the baby. Jade misses having Mummy all to herself, and that's okay."

'The more opportunities children have to put a label on emotions, and the more they see that all emotions are normal and accepted, the easier they will find it to communicate their own feelings.'

Sal, who is a mother to two young children, also shared with me a brilliant, playful activity for helping younger children express and identify mixed emotions.

Playdough emotions

- Decide on a few different emotions, and a different colour of playdough to represent each one.
- Draw a simple face to show each emotion, and place a blob of each colour dough by each face. This will be your reference chart.
- Discuss a scenario with your child, factual or hypothetical, and then identify together which emotions they might feel.
- Take colours and quantities of play dough that accurately represent how they feel — for example, being home from school might be half sad (missing friends), a quarter happy (spending more time with family), and a little bit worried and excited.

- Squish them together and mix them up to demonstrate that we can feel lots of different emotions all at the same time.

Positive communication

Everything we've explored so far — understanding the roots of our children's behaviour, rethinking punishments and rewards as parenting techniques, building connection during times of uncertainty, learning from our children's play — can be boiled down to one thing: communication. Communication is the foundation of everything we do as parents.

We want the way we communicate with our children to teach them that they are worth listening to, and that it is safe for them to express their emotions. To do this, we may have to unlearn patterns of communication we learnt in our own childhoods.

Calm communication is as much about a shift in *thinking* as a shift in language, allowing you to move from a place of judgement, anger, or frustration ('He is doing it on purpose to annoy me! How did I raise such an entitled brat?') to a place of compassion and empathy, where you seek to understand the motivations of those around you ('He must be having a really hard time to be acting like that, I wonder what's upsetting him?'). Being thoughtful about communication is the cornerstone of calm parenting. It can move you away from automatic reactions which further add to the conflict in your home — shouting, threatening, and shaming your child for their behaviour — towards more thoughtful responses which seek to understand.

Treating your child as a person first and foremost, and talking to them as you would an adult who you trust and respect, can radically change how you communicate with them. Think about how you like being spoken to. Your children are no different!

Respectful communication might look like:

Being honest with your children about how you are feeling.

For example, giving them an explanation when you are feeling tired, stressed, or grumpy, just as you might another adult.

Not interrupting your children or talking over them.

Listening carefully when they speak, and taking what they say — their ideas, suggestions, concerns, feelings, advice, requests — seriously, rather than dismissing them.

Not rushing in with solutions straightaway.

If your child mentions a problem or worry, it can be tempting to dive in with a suggestion or solution. But keeping that impulse in check, holding space for them to share, and gently empathising ('I can see that felt really hurtful') and asking open questions ('So, what do you think you could do?') helps your child to build confidence around figuring out their own solutions to their problems, and encourages resilience and emotional literacy.

Using positive language.

Rather than telling your child what they may not do, reframe your request in terms of what they may do. This is effective because our children hear what we would like them to do, rather than hearing what we would not like them to do. When we say, 'You can't run in the house,' our child still hears the words 'run in the house', which emphasises the very thing we are trying to discourage! Instead, try reframing it as, 'Running is for outdoors.' It also gives them an alternative course of action, rather than just telling them what we don't like.

Telling them what you are doing and taking their consent seriously (e.g. stopping if they say 'stop').

With a very young child this might look like telling your baby that you are about to pick them up, or change their nappy, or wipe their face, or put them in the buggy. It might be about explaining to your toddler that they are going to have a vaccine which will hurt but will stop them getting unwell in the long run, or that you're going to need to put them in the car seat because otherwise the car isn't a safe place to be. It might look like talking to your pre-schooler about why their teeth need to be brushed, or trusting them when they say they've had enough to eat. And with a teenager, it might mean listening to them when they tell you that they don't want a hug — no matter how hard this can be to hear. It means talking clearly to your child about what you want to do to them and why, and truly listening to them and engaging with them if and when they say no.

Acknowledging their worries, thoughts, and feelings with empathy and kindness.

(Even if they seem unimportant to you!)

Saying yes more than you say no.

When children hear 'no' all the time, it starts to lose its meaning. It's better to save 'no' for serious situations where you really need your child to pay attention urgently. You can instead reframe your message in a positive way; for example, 'No, you can't have that teddy' might become, 'Yes, we can put it on your birthday list', or 'No more biscuits' might become 'You can have another one tomorrow'. Before saying no, you can also consider why you want to say no — would saying yes be genuinely harmful to your child?

Developing calm, respectful communication skills takes work; like any new skill, practice makes it infinitely easier. But it is certainly a skill worth practising, as once you start to shift how you communicate with your children you will notice radical transformation in your relationship. A great, practical approach to this kind of communication is Nonviolent Communication.

Nonviolent Communication

Nonviolent Communication (NVC) is an approach developed by Marshall Rosenberg, and made popular in his book *Nonviolent Communication,* where he states:

'NVC guides us in reframing how we express ourselves

and hear others. Instead of habitual, automatic reactions, our words are conscious responses based firmly on awareness of what we are perceiving, feeling, and wanting.'

The core idea behind Nonviolent Communication is that everything we do, we do to get our needs met. When this thinking is applied to others, it makes it much easier to empathise. And when it comes to parenting, this requires a shift away from evaluating children in terms such as naughty/good or right/wrong to a language based around their needs. It helps us to see that our children's communication — be it through actions or words — is valuable, even in the challenging moments.

The Nonviolent Communication process uses four components: observation, feelings, needs, and requests. Let's look at these in a little more detail:

Observations.

The first step is to observe what is happening. What are we observing others doing or saying that we like or do not like? Then, we need to be able to express this observation without judgement or evaluation. This sounds simple, but can be surprisingly hard to do. For example, 'She is a terrible sleeper' or 'He is lazy' are evaluations, but 'She woke up five times last night' or 'He often does his homework late' are observations. When we communicate our evaluations rather than our observations, it makes it much less likely that our requests will be met with a positive response — no one likes to feel labelled or judged.

Feelings.

Once we have communicated our observations, we can follow up with how we are feeling. Here again, we need to make a distinction between evaluations masquerading as feelings ('I feel like I'm living with a tiny tyrant!') and our actual feelings ('I feel exhausted and frustrated'). Expressing our feelings allows us to show vulnerability, and removes the focus from the other person or situation and places it back on us. This focus on us rather than on others is important when talking about our feelings, as it encourages us to take responsibility for our feelings. Yes, the actions of others can cause emotional reactions in us, but no one can *make* us feel something. There is a big difference between 'You make me feel so angry' and 'I am feeling really angry right now'.

The more precise we can be about our feelings, the better.

Needs.

Once we have expressed our observation and our feelings, we can share the needs behind our feelings. For example, 'When I see you hit your sister, I feel scared because I need to keep her safe' or 'When you leave your dirty dishes in the sink rather than putting them in the dishwasher, I feel exasperated. I need to feel respected and like we are on the same team.' Often, we mistake communicating our observations and feelings with communicating our needs, but these are very different. For example, we might say 'I feel tired' to our partner when really we want to be communicating a need ('I need more time to rest'), then end up frustrated when our needs are not acknowledged or met.

Requests.

Finally, once we have communicated our observation, feelings, and need, we can make a request. The word request here is important: when we are making a request of someone — be it our partner, our child, or our parent — we have to leave open the possibility that they will choose to say no. If this is not the case — if there is no option to decline — then we are not making a request, we are making a demand. Again, the difference is subtle, but it is important. When people perceive that we are making a demand rather than a request, there are only two possible responses: submission or rebellion. Neither of these scenarios makes the person feel like they have much freedom of choice! When making requests, it also helps to keep these requests specific (not 'I need more help' but 'Would you be willing to set the table for me?'). Sometimes we will need to make a demand: not hitting a sibling, touching a stove, or running into the road is far more than a request. But in these circumstances, which are usually urgent and to do with safety, we will usually step in immediately so this approach wouldn't be helpful in any case; you're not going to say 'I observe you walking close to the stove with your hand out, and I feel worried' — you're going to block your child from burning themselves.

I would also add a fifth element to this list: **Empathy**. Let the person you're talking to know that you also care about how they feel, and that you're keeping their needs in mind, too. I've found this to be so important, whether I'm talking to my husband about how we can balance chores with our busy work schedules and homeschooling, or whether I'm talking to my daughter about why I really don't want her to keep banging her drum when I have a headache. Trying to understand the situation from their perspective keeps conflict down and paves the way for mutual understanding.

It may seem unnatural to change the way you talk to your child at first — you might like to try out a few different ways of saying things until you find one that sounds more like you. Don't be too worried about getting it wrong; remember, you are the expert on your child and will have an instinctive understanding of the kinds of expressions that will resonate for them.

When words are not enough

Sometimes when you are asking a young child to stop doing something — or asking them to do something — simply speaking to them is not enough, and you need to actually show them what is required, and then help them to follow through. For example, if you are asking them to put their shoes away, you can instead go over to them, walk with them to the shoe storage, and show them where their shoes should go.

When you need to communicate something to your child, but they are busy doing something else, rather than calling out, go over to them, make eye contact, reach out to them, and wait for a moment to tell them whatever it is you need to say. It makes sense to give your child opportunities for success when it comes to communication, and this increases the chances of your child taking in what you need them to hear.

This is especially important when it comes to enforcing your well-considered limits. For example, rather than telling your child not to hit or push another child (which they are not doing because they love hitting or pushing, but rather because they are struggling with something), you can immediately step in and, if necessary, gently remove your child from the situation.

Helping your child to immediately stop any harmful behaviour is not just good for those around them, but it's also much kinder to your own child as it stops the behaviour before you have a chance to start feeling frustrated or annoyed at them.

Changing the way you communicate will come with time and practice; even if you think about calm parenting consciously once a day, it will still feed into everything you are doing on a subconscious level.

I know that working on the way you communicate with your child can feel like an irrelevant luxury when times are tough. It can feel like all you can do is focus on getting through the days, and that you don't have the energy to think about parenting. I get it. But, paradoxically, it's exactly during challenging times, when emotions can run high and everyone feels worn out, that communicating precisely and empathically can be of most value. We see this most clearly when our children are having a really hard time, culminating in tantrums.

Supporting your child through strong feelings and navigating tantrums

If there's one word guaranteed to make parents shudder, it's the T-word: tantrum. Tantrums can be intensely difficult for parents to navigate, bringing up a cocktail of potent feelings: sadness, anger, frustration, worry, shame. It can be especially hard if you're in public and you find yourself on the receiving end of judgement or unkindness from passers-by; more than one of my clients have had people tutting at them as they tried to console an inconsolable child in a carpark or supermarket.

The good news is that tantrums are normal and perfectly healthy. They are a way some children — not just toddlers! — express feelings of intense emotion, frustration, anger, or upset. They help children regulate their emotions and let off steam in the only way they know how, as they are unable to filter their emotions and control their feelings in the same way most adults can. Think about how good it can feel to have a proper cry when things feel hard. Don't you feel better afterwards? Children are the same! The space to express themselves without shame — even if that means screaming on the floor of the supermarket — is one of the best gifts we can give them.

Tantrums are normal at the best of times, but when you are going through a period of uncertainly, you can expect to see more tantrums, big feelings, and challenging behaviours as your children process and find ways to cope with unfamiliarity, change, and familial stress.

Witnessing your children sharing these big, overwhelming feelings may bring up a powerful emotional response and can make you feel panicked ('Why can't I get through to my child?'), upset ('She told me she wants me to go away and she hates me'), or even angry ('I am so tired and work so hard for my child, and he repays me by screaming at me?'). This may be especially hard if the space to express your emotions was not held for you by your parents — perhaps they told you to stop crying when you were sad, or shut down expressions of anger, or you were told to be a 'big girl' when you were disappointed. (Dan Siegel and Mary Hartzell's book *Parenting from the Inside Out* is a brilliant read if you want to understand how the way you were parented can shape your responses as a parent.) The emotions you feel may mean that holding the space for your child to express themselves with all of their messy, raw, but important human emotions can leave you exhausted and emotionally vulnerable. If possible, find time later to speak to someone — your partner, your mum, a good friend — about how you felt, or take five minutes to journal about it.

As well as debriefing afterwards, there are also some steps you can take in the heat of the moment to calm the situation. Here are some key techniques for coping with tantrums:

Stay physically present.

Some children will tolerate being held or cuddled while experiencing feelings of overwhelm, but some will not want to be touched. In this case, stay close by and use words to remind your child you are there: 'I'm here for you, I'm ready to give you a hug when you feel ready.'

Keep everyone safe.

That includes the child who is experiencing strong emotions, any other children around, and yourself. 'I see you really want to hit — I will stop you hitting your brother.'

Hold to your limits.

It is important for you to maintain your family's thought-through, necessary limits — and it is also okay for your child to be upset at these boundaries. 'I won't buy you a second ice cream. It's okay for you to be angry with me, I know how much you wanted it.'

Offer an alternative to words for your child to express themselves.

A piece of paper for drawing their emotions, a cushion for punching or kicking, a beanbag to throw, or some playdough to squeeze — these are all ways for a child to vent some of the frustration they are feeling in a way that doesn't require words.

Don't dwell on it.

If you allow your child to safely work through their emotions, they will often feel calm and even happy once the feelings have passed, as though they have got everything out of their system and are ready to move on. Offer a cuddle, check that they are okay, then move on, too.

Sportscasting

Sportscasting — a term coined by infant specialist Magda Gerber (1910–2007) to mean judgement-free, factual narration — is a great way of supporting your child through a challenging situation, either alone ('You dropped your cracker and it broke, and now you are feeling sad') or when in conflict with another child ('I can see that you both want to play with that car, but Jane is playing and it doesn't look like she is finished with it'). It is simply describing what you see happening in a non-judgemental, calm manner.

Sportscasting offers children the space to come up with their own solutions or work through conflicts to reach a solution. This demonstrates trust: it says to them, 'I'm right here if you need me, but I trust you to manage this.' It also encourages children to come up with a mutually acceptable solution themselves ('Okay, so John has the ball, but you both want to play with it. What do you think we should do?'), allowing them to develop problem-solving and communication skills.

Labelling emotions through sportscasting ('You keep trying to fit the car into the box but it's not fitting. I can see that it's making you frustrated') can give children the language to express how they are feeling.

How to keep yourself calm during tricky times

Being the calm in the storm when your child is raging is hard, there are no two ways about it. But there are things you can do to give yourself a fighting chance:

Breathe.

Take some deep breaths, counting slowly to ten, before responding. Relax your shoulders. It's amazing how effective just pausing for a moment is when it comes to helping us respond empathically and peacefully rather than reacting in a way which doesn't feel good.

Remember you are the adult.

When you feel your frustration building, take a moment to ask yourself, 'If I am an adult and I feel frustrated and am finding this moment hard, how might my child be feeling?'

Text an understanding friend or partner.

Just because you don't want to take your frustration out on your child, it doesn't mean you need to bottle it up. The very act of offloading can help us feel better and calmer (and reminds us we are the adult), and if we are lucky, the adult connection and empathy we receive back further supports us to stay calm and gain some perspective on the situation.

Make sure everyone is fed, hydrated, well rested, and at a comfortable temperature — including you.

It's amazing how tensions and frustrations can be eliminated with a well-timed glass of water, slice of buttered toast, jumper, or mug of hot chocolate.

Remind yourself that your child's behaviour is not a reflection on you as a parent.

Behaviour is how children communicate and process emotions and feelings; it can tell us a lot about a child's needs, but nothing about how loving a parent you are.

What to do when you've lost your cool

Sometimes with the best will in the world, you just can't stay calm and you end up shouting, threatening, or acting in other ways which don't make you feel proud. If this happens, there are always things you can do to recover the situation:

Take a moment.

If you feel out of control, take a time-out (always making sure your child is safe, of course). Scream into a pillow. Drink a cup of tea. Eat some chocolate. Whatever you need to do to return to your child calmly.

Apologise.

Say sorry to your child. This is so important and so powerful. Being able to admit when we are wrong and give our child the respect of a heartfelt apology is one of the most important things we can do and model as parents.

Reconnect.

This might be through physical means, such as a cuddle or some roughhousing, or by doing something together such as reading a book, playing a game, or going for a walk. Focus on your child, give them your attention, show them with your actions that you love them and that they are safe.

Forgive yourself.

You are only human, and you are not perfect. It's easy to let tough moments cast a shadow on the day, or to start thinking, 'I am a terrible parent, I'm such a failure, why can't I keep calm?' but try to recognise those thoughts and then nip them in the bud. Tomorrow is a new day.

Take some time to reflect.

What could have triggered your child's challenging behaviour — were any needs not being met? What could have triggered your reaction to that behaviour?

Make time for self-care.

Losing patience with our children is often a sign that our own needs are not being met; it is so much harder to respond with empathy and patience when we are running on empty ourselves. Remember that your needs are just as important and valid as your child's, and make it a priority to look after yourself physically and emotionally.

Connecting through nonverbal communication

Positive nonverbal communication can build and boost your emotional connection with your children. Warm and caring body language — touching their arm, offering a hug, giving kisses — sends the nonverbal message that you want to be close to your child.

Get down to their level.

Crouch or sit down next to them, and make eye contact when you are speaking to them. If this is not possible (you're doing the washing-up, for example), then turn to look at them.

Use consensual touch.

A hand on their arm shows them that you are focused on them and offers closeness. Offer physical affection such as hugs, cuddles, and kisses liberally, but also respect your child's wishes if they don't want to be touched right now.

Pay attention to your facial expressions.

For example, making a 'yuck' face when changing a nappy communicates to your child that they are disgusting.

Mirror your child.

Mirroring their expressions and body language shows them that you are attuned to them, and take them seriously. Using open body language (arms open, leaning towards your child), rather than closed (arms or legs crossed, leaning away), is also more reassuring, especially if you're at their height

Be mindful of distractions.

Put your phone on airplane mode, turn off the radio, put your book down. Studies have shown that when parents check their devices, this has a negative effect on children's ability to sustain attention (Yu & Smith, 2016) and learn new information (Hirsh-Pasek, Reed & Golinkoff, 2017).

The inner work of parenting

As we have seen in this chapter, when it comes down to it, peaceful parenting is very much about us as parents, and not much at all about our children. It's not about trying to find 'gentle' ways to discipline our children, or getting them to comply with our wishes without tears, or fit into our schedules. It's about working on ourselves as humans so that we can live as happily and peacefully with the younger humans that we share our lives with as possible, to everyone's benefit. We will come back to looking at the self-work of parenting and how you can create the right conditions for it in Chapter Five. In the meantime, let's look at how your own emotions and history influence your parenting style.

When we stop trying to change our children's behaviour and instead focus on being aware, present, and mindful of our own behaviour, amazing things can happen. But I'm not going to pretend this is easy. Working on ourselves as parents often means digging into our own experiences of childhood, our struggles, and our insecurities. This 'inner work' encourages us to confront our beliefs and our fears, and to work actively to reprogram our parenting autopilot, which so often kicks in when we are triggered, tired, stressed, or upset.

If you have other things on your mind, it might feel like focusing on this challenging inner work is the last thing you have time for. But it's precisely at times like these that we need to be thinking about how we are showing up as parents.

If uncertainly and change is hard for us, it's hard for our children too. They pick up on things — the whispers and news clips — and any departure from secure and comforting rhythms means that your children are going to need you to be the calm in the storm. You will need to prepare yourself for big feelings and emotional outbursts, and for behaviour which challenges and triggers you. You will need to dig deep to remember that all behaviour is communication, and that sometimes your children are going to be communicating, 'I feel scared. I feel worried. Things are unpredictable. I feel uneasy.' It's precisely at these times that your children need, more than ever, for you to seek to understand that language, and respond with empathy and kindness, with creativity and love.

This is the gift that this inner work can offer your family.

Identifying your parenting triggers

Our interactions with our own children are so tied up with our own experiences of childhood. Because of this, our children's actions can often trigger intense feelings of frustration, powerlessness, and anger in us. But it is possible to learn to identify these triggers, move past them, and even learn from them.

Triggers are words, phrases, or actions that cause us to react and feel strong emotion — usually negative. These are often connected to painful or challenging experiences from our past. When we experience a strong response to our children's behaviour — for example, whining or shouting — it is usually about our own difficulty in processing these emotions rather than our child's behaviour itself.

In the words of Teresa Graham Brett in her book *Parenting for Social Change*:

'Triggers are often a sign of unintegrated emotional experiences that are a result of emotional control we may have experienced as children. Often when we are triggered by something a child says or does, it brings up emotions that are related to an incident earlier in our lives where we experienced pain. On our parenting journey, these triggers can be insight into our experiences of powerlessness as a child that are now impacting how we interact with the children in our lives. If these reactions remain unexamined, we miss an opportunity to move through the emotions still following, maybe even haunting us, from our past.'

Paying attention to the moments when you feel most triggered can often lead to reflection on your own experiences as a child. It's not unusual to realise that you feel triggered by the very behaviour that you were reprimanded, shamed, or punished for as a child (jumping on sofas, throwing food, dawdling, crying, saying no to parents). This situational trigger takes you back to how you felt as a child: powerless, hurt, or ashamed.

The good news? It is absolutely possible to learn to identity your triggers, and better anticipate when you may feel triggered by a situation. This is powerful work, and can lead to a fresh sense of self-awareness.

It can be really useful to keep a 'trigger diary' in a small notebook or by emailing yourself a quick note. Each time you feel triggered — a strong emotional reaction which makes it hard to respond calmly to your child — make a note of what was happening, how you were feeling before, any external factors (for example, too hot, thirsty), any emotional and physical feelings that came up for you afterwards, and if you have a sense of where these feelings may have originated (it's okay if you don't). It can be difficult at first to isolate what is feeling triggered vs feeling frustrated, tired, hot, or hungry, but when you start paying attention to your feelings you'll see a difference in how triggering behaviour makes us feel: overwhelmed, irrational, and out of control with regard to our parenting.

Keeping a diary allows you to spot patterns in your feelings and begin to anticipate and perhaps avoid situations which could trigger these emotional responses. You may also begin to find that just by focusing on how you are feeling, these feelings slowly begin to feel less overwhelming and you are able to respond mindfully more often.

Developing self-awareness

Awareness requires us to observe how our beliefs and behaviours impact other people and ourselves. Developing awareness as a parent requires us to begin understanding who we are, what is important to us, what we believe about our children and childhood, and how we relate to the world around us.

Developing awareness in our parenting prompts us to ask ourselves:

- What impact do my actions have on my child? How will they shape the person they are growing into?
- How do my actions right now fit with my values and beliefs?
- What am I finding challenging? When do I feel frustrated? Fearful? Insecure? Overwhelmed? How can I support myself through these feelings? What do I need from myself right now? What are these feelings telling me?
- How have my childhood experiences influenced my view of children, childhood, and the role of parents?
- What is my child really asking of me right now, through their being and their behaviour?

A big part of this inner work is accepting that you are not perfect — no one is. Every parent will make mistakes, have bad days, react in haste rather than taking time to respond, and lose their temper. I am a peaceful-parenting coach and I still lose my cool sometimes! Rather than turning these moments into a source of guilt and shame, and dwelling on them, you can offer yourself kind acceptance and a willingness to grow and learn from these difficult moments (we will be looking at this self-compassion more in Chapter

Five). Something powerful I tell myself is that, if I could have acted differently, I would have done. This allows for kindness towards myself, while still acknowledging that I would like to have acted differently.

It is often the hardest moments in our parenting journey that bring us the most growth, learning, and wisdom, and the deepest opportunities for developing awareness. Although at the time it might be hard to see what positives the hard situation we face could ever bring, this growth is often felt when the crisis is over and we move back towards peace and equilibrium.

Calm in the Storm summary

- Attachment and connection are at the heart of a healthy parent–child relationship. Moving away from shame-based parenting methods and responding to your child's emotional and physical needs can strengthen this attachment, no matter how old your child is, or your previous parenting methods.
- Behaviour is always a form of communication. When you pay attention to what is going on under the surface, you can connect with your children with empathy while still setting loving limits around behaviour.
- Tantrums are normal and healthy, although they pose a challenge to us as parents.
- Changing how you communicate with your children won't be easy, but it's one of the best ways to build a positive, respectful relationship with them.
- Being playful with your children helps strengthen their emotional development, and is more effective than punitive discipline, strengthening connection and dissolving conflict and tension in the home
- Working on yourself as a parent — noticing your triggers and developing self-awareness and self-compassion — is more valuable and important than trying to change your children's behaviour.
- There's no such thing as a perfect parent. You are doing your best.

Chapter Two

Rhythm in the home

Children thrive on predictability and flow. But how can you provide this stability when the world around you feels like it's at its most unpredictable? Enter your secret weapon: the family rhythm.

Children often have little control over what happens in their lives; over where they need to be, what they are allowed to do, and what rules and limits are enforced. Infants are picked up and moved with no warning, toddlers bundled into the car at a moment's notice, school-age children told they can't watch more TV on a weekday when they're used to watching it at the weekend, teens given seemingly arbitrary curfews — children of all ages often have limited input into the structure of their days. But having a strong rhythm, where daily life flows in a predictable way, can provide welcome security and comfort, a sense of 'I am safe because I know what comes next', and an understanding of 'this is what we do', be it taking dishes to the sink after each meal or going to the park every Wednesday after breakfast.

When you reflect on your own childhood, what are the events that you remember best? Maybe it was a daily occurrence, like being picked up by your grandma from school or having a story read to you before bed. Or it could have been a weekly ritual like Sunday lunch, doing an after-school activity each Thursday, or having a special treat you were only allowed at the weekend. Or perhaps it's seasonal events you think of first — harvest celebrations or Thanksgiving, religious festivals like Christmas, Diwali, Eid, or Hannukah, or big family barbecues during summer. Each of these memories are part of the rhythms of your own childhood, and will have their own sets of associations — smells, foods, sensations, and emotions. Remembering how they made you feel as a child can help you identify the kinds of rhythms you would like to create for your child, and reveal the power that lies behind consistency and repetition.

I first discovered the magic of rhythm when I signed up to a Waldorf parent and child class with my daughter Frida when she was a toddler. Each week we would attend the London Steiner School for two blissful hours, the strong rhythm of the class gently guiding the children through play, snack, songs, and stories. They were the most relaxing two hours of the week, and when our group leader explained that rhythm can help children feel less overwhelmed and more in control as they navigate life and learn what is expected of them, it made perfect sense. And it's exactly when life is at its most unpredictable that children benefit from rhythm the most.

Owner of holistic parenting business and blog Whole Family Rhythms, and mother of four, Meagan Wilson agrees:

'Daily, weekly, and seasonal rhythms are the anchors which provide security and happiness to children. With a strong daily rhythm, a child knows what to expect and what is expected. With rhythm, simple daily activities — chores, self-care, meal times — become habits instead of arguments.'

It's not just children who benefit from more predictability and stability in their lives. As parents, living in a more rhythmic way can help us to simplify our lives and focus on what matters most. And of course, reducing conflict around things like bedtime, screen-time, and chores all helps to reduce parental stress levels! Personally, I have found implementing a family rhythm transformational in bringing more ease and joy into my daily life as a parent to a young child. I hope that you find crafting a rhythm as positive an experience as our family did.

Rhythm, not routine

One of the questions I'm most often asked when it comes to family rhythms is, 'Are you not just describing a routine? What's the difference?' But whereas the words routine and schedule conjure up images of timetables, with minutes and hours strictly allocated to different tasks, rhythm is about creating days which flow in a predictable way.

We have a bedtime rhythm for our daughter, which means she has a bath after dinner but before brushing her teeth. The bath usually happens around seven o'clock, but it might be a little earlier, or later, depending on how our day has been. Some days she has a bath in the afternoon and skips one before bed altogether. This means bedtime is predictable, but we don't feel stressed or worried if it differs slightly from day to day. Rhythm is there to be a helpful guide rather than a taskmaster, and it can and should be flexible. It's there to serve your needs, not to hold you to times and activities which don't suit you or your family.

Chances are you probably already have rhythms in place. If you have young children, they probably go to bed roughly at the same time every evening, following loosely the same predictable pattern of activities: bath, pyjamas, snack, teeth, story, kiss, lights out. They might not do this at seven-thirty on the dot, and some nights you might read for longer than others, but you still have a rhythm in place that calms your child, provides connection, and prepares them for sleep. And even with older children, you likely have a consistent pattern of saying goodnight, who switches the light off, and how long they are allowed to read in bed.

Meagan continues: 'When you first set about planning your daily rhythm, it is always important to focus on your family values. What is it you want to animate on a daily basis and why is this important to you?'

Rhythm allows us to live in alignment with what matters to us, and it teaches our children that these things matter, through regular repetition. Like it or not, how we live our daily lives teaches our children a great deal about what we believe matters the most. Let's explore the idea of values a little further.

Identifying your family's needs and values

Identifying your parenting values

In my popular online course Rhythm in the Home, the first thing I ask my clients to do is to explore the idea of values. Your values are, simply put, the things that you believe to be important to the way you live your life. They could be moral or ethical principles, or they might highlight something else that is important to you as a family.

Many of the parents I work with have never had the time or opportunity to reflect on how their values show up in their parenting before — as parents, life can be so busy that we often don't take the time to reflect on our parenting unless something has gone wrong — and doing so can be enlightening. It might feel like a luxury you simply don't have time for. But I promise, it's worth making some space to explore what's important to you, because once you have built a strong foundation, your rhythm can ebb and flow while still keeping the essential core of what makes it work for your family.

I ask my clients a series of questions to help them define their parenting values; you might like to write your answers down, discuss them with your partner or a friend, or just reflect upon them as you go about your daily life.

- When have you felt happiest? What was present in these moments?
- When have you felt the most pride? What contributed to this feeling?
- When have you felt most frustrated and unfulfilled? What was lacking in these moments?
- What are your hopes for the world? Name five things that you believe make for a good and happy society.

Now let's dig a little deeper into what is important for you when it comes to parenting your children:

- Think about some times that have felt good for you as a family. What were you doing? What was present? How did you show up as a parent? How did your relationship with your children feel? How do you think your children felt?
- If you could gift five characteristics or qualities to your children as they grow up, what would they be?
- Is there anything from your own childhood that you would like to pass down to your children?
- How would you like your children to describe you when they are grown? List any words that come up.
- What would a beautiful childhood look like to you?

Once you've answered these questions, look for recurring words or phrases which jump out at you. Your values might change a little each time you do this exercise; that's okay, they're just reflecting your needs and priorities in that moment.

The reason I always start with this work is that, when we are clear about what's important to us, it allows us to critically assess our current lives. If 'time in nature' is something you value, but you barely make it to the park once a week, perhaps this is something that needs rebalancing. Perhaps you're even putting a lot of time and effort into another activity that isn't particularly important to you, through sheer force of habit. Gaining clarity around what's truly important to you as a parent for yourself and your family is hugely valuable in guiding the decisions and choices you make. But it's not just your values that will guide your rhythm, but your family's unique needs too.

Identifying your family's needs

Taking some time to think about what you and your family need to be happy and fulfilled is also important when thinking about what a good, strong, flexible rhythm might look like. When your rhythm is shaped by your family's needs, those needs have more chance of getting met, and understanding them is the key to creating a rhythm which truly works for you and your child, rather than following a cookie-cutter schedule which is designed for someone who lives a very different life to you.

- What do you need to keep yourself feeling happy, healthy, and able to look after your family? Do you need time alone, or do you recharge your batteries by socialising? What does self-care look like for you? Do you get enough of it? If not, why not? What would you like more of?
- Think about each of your children. What do they need at the moment? Forget external expectations for a moment and think about them as individuals. What do they need to be happy? Are they introverted or extroverted? What keeps them feeling good? If you have more than one child, where can both have their needs met together, and where do their needs conflict?
- Think about your partner, if you have one. What makes them feel happy, healthy, and replenished? What needs to be in place for your relationship to thrive?

Making space to think about what each of you needs — as individuals and as a family unit — will make for a more harmonious family life, decreasing conflict and increasing joy and connection. This can be especially useful in challenging times when it can feel harder to get basic needs met.

Daily rhythms

When you are at home with your children full-time, whether you are home educating them or not, daily rhythms become particularly important. What your days look like will depend a lot on your children's requirements — and your own. A strong, flexible daily rhythm can take a little while to figure out and get used to. But I promise, once you're in the habit of following a family rhythm, you won't look back.

I spoke to Pippa Hounslow, a busy self-employed mother of three young children aged five, three, and one, about why she uses a daily rhythm:

'I think my whole family benefit from our daily rhythm, but no one more than me. It takes an element of stress out of planning and keeps days manageable; if we base our days around a few key activities such as "crafts" and "outside time" it gives us enough freedom to change it up and keep them fresh. If I'm calm and ready for the day, I think that has a positive effect on everyone around me.'

Breathing in, breathing out

In the Waldorf philosophy, the breathing-in phase refers to a period of time when you are connecting with your child. This might be reading, playing together, chatting, sharing a meal, or being present with your attention while your child paints or builds. The breathing-out phase refers to a period of time when your child relates mainly to the world around them (independent free play, running around the park, writing a letter to a friend). For each breathing-in period, the child needs a breathing-out period, and so a pattern is established; breathing-in tops up the child's connection with you and fills them up, so that they can then spend time without your full attention as you breathe out.

As we explored in Chapter One, when children feel lonely, or a loss of connection, this is often expressed in behaviour which challenges us as parents and leads to conflict or stress. Loosely following this pattern of 'in breath, out breath' in the home can help you build up regular connection with your child, and reduce feelings of stress for you both. Older children and teenagers may need less breathing-in time throughout the day, but they will still need moments of connection with you. And having this pattern in mind for those moments of stress can serve as a reminder to reach out and connect with your child when things feel tough.

Example rhythm for daily life at home with young children

Here is an example of what a daily rhythm might look like with young children (0–7) in the home; your rhythm may look totally different, and that's fine!

- Wake up, toilet/nappy, make beds.
- Play while breakfast is prepared and last night's laundry

hung up, tidy toys, wash hands. This could also be a good time for a yoga video.

- Gather for breakfast, sharing your hopes for the day and lighting a candle. Linger at the table to read a poem and some books.
- Wash hands, clear table, everyone gets dressed, teeth and hair brushed.
- Outside in park, nature walk, or garden/play at home.
- Home for lunch (following meal rhythm).
- Nap/quiet time for children; some time to unwind for parent.
- Play together.
- Daily activity: art, baking, gardening, playdough, watch a film.
- Tea time with snack and some books.
- Chores — tidying, cleaning, preparing evening meal. Children can help or play.
- Evening meal.
- Bedtime rhythm.

If your child usually attends school or childcare but has had to leave at short notice, it can be comforting to try to replicate a similar rhythm at home. I don't mean strictly following their old timetable, but rather keeping similar times for meals, weaving in any beloved activities (if they learnt Spanish on Wednesdays then perhaps you could continue at home), and video-calling friends before lunchtime to say hello when they would usually be playing. Keeping a thread of predictability running through their days as they adapt to their new rhythm will be key in helping them feel secure and relaxed.

Rhythm is still important for older children and teenagers, but instead of building a rhythm yourself, you can involve them in the process — be prepared to entertain a range of views on what that might look like! Family rhythm with older children will likely look less structured on a day-by-day basis, but you might still keep anchors around family meals, a regular family film night, or set times for more formal learning or work to happen.

Anchors

Anchors are the points in your day that your rhythm hangs onto. Whatever else happens, whatever might be going on, whatever changes are needed, having consistent anchor points holds your rhythm together, and can bring a lot of comfort and joy to both you and your children. The best thing about anchors is that they are already there in your life waiting for you to use them!

I spoke to Kelly Ellis-Radahd, a Steiner early-childhood educator and mother to three children, about why having a rhythm is essential for her family:

'For our family — three children with large age gaps, aged one, eight, and twelve — rhythm nourishes us as individuals and celebrates us as a family. It allows us time to follow and meet our own varying interests and needs, and then brings us together to share in the same beat through times such as meal times and outdoor walks. When kept simple with moments to breathe separately and then come together, a nourishing rhythm can provide children of all ages with time and energy to be full participants in their own learning and share in the joys of others.'

Meal times, the start of the day, and bedtime can work really well as anchors to build strong rhythms around, as these always have to happen day in, day out. Let's look at each of these in a little more detail.

Meal times

When making your home more rhythmic, meals are a perfect place to start. No matter what's going on around you, everyone has to eat, and meals provide a regular anchor point for the rest of your day. Although meal times with young children can sometimes feel chaotic and thankless, the repetition and rhythm built around them slowly becomes habitual and children accept them as 'the way we do things'.

You could consider:

- Asking children to help. Younger children might lay the table or fill up water glasses at the beginning of each meal, and carry their dishes to the sink after the meal has ended, whereas teens might be in charge of cooking the whole meal once a week or contribute to discussions about meal plans.
- Introducing set meals for each day of the week — pasta night, soup night, pizza night. Within each theme there's still room for variation, and it saves a surprising amount of mental energy.
- Batch cooking once a week (roasting veg, meat, prepping fruit and raw veg for snacks) while listening to podcasts or music.

- Lighting a candle at the start of each meal, and blowing or snuffing it out at the end.
- For younger children, washing hands at the start and end of each meal (you could sing, 'This is how we wash our hands, wash our hands ...').
- For infants, singing a simple little song at the start of each milky meal. (I should say here that I recommend feeding babies on demand, whether they are breast- or bottle-fed, unless there is medical advice not to do so.)
- Putting distractions away during meals and sharing conversation that the whole family can participate in.
- Sharing poems, rhymes, verses, prayers, or blessings — whatever fits with your family's beliefs and values.
- Building in a gratitude practice by each sharing one thing you are thankful for (with young children you can talk about something they feel happy about). With older children, once a week you could go round the table and each share one highlight and one challenge of the week just gone.

Bedtimes

If you have young children, bedtimes are another good place to start when crafting strong daily rhythms, and again form an excellent daily anchor point, a point of calm at the end of a long day. Keeping bedtimes consistent and predictable, with the same things happening in the same order — no matter who is putting your child to bed — helps your child to feel secure and wind down. If your children still nap, consider having a pared-down nap rhythm as well, even if it's just drawing the curtains and singing a song.

You could consider:

- Including a bath or shower to help your child wind down.
- Lighting a candle for bedtime which is blown out as a symbolic act of saying goodnight, or switching on a nightlight if they find it hard to relax in the dark.
- Using a few drops of lavender essential oil or another familiar smell to help your child relax.
- Giving your child a gentle massage before bed.
- Introducing a bedtime snack — porridge, warm milk, or a slice of toast. Even if they have already eaten supper, for some children this seems to be helpful.
- Saying goodnight to toys.
- Blowing dreams or goodnight wishes into your child's ears.
- Listening to a night-time meditation for children.
- Offering a story (read or told) before bed, being consistent with how many you offer each night.
- Laying out clothes the night before, especially if you have a child that struggles with morning transitions.

Even with teenagers, you might still have a rhythm where you go in and say goodnight to them each night, providing a dependable space and time for them to share anything they might have on their mind.

Starting the day

Starting the day can often feel chaotic. But because mornings will usually share the same elements day in and day out, they can be a great place to insert more rhythm. For many of us, mornings are not when we are at our best, and stressful mornings can feel doubly fraught because they hold a mirror up to parts of us we don't like — perhaps we wish we were more organised, or more able to get up early and prep before the children wake up.

However, even if you're decidedly not a morning person, there are some things you can do to bring a little more ease and joy into the morning routine.

- Think about first thing. How do the children wake up? If you wake them, do you do this in a way which is likely to lead to feelings of calm? Can you take a moment to lie together, sharing your dreams or talking about what you look forward to that day? If they wake up by themselves, are you ready to greet them when they do so?
- Focus on your own morning routine. Getting your own morning started off right so that you can show up to your parenting duties feeling calm (this might mean gritting your teeth and setting an alarm before the children wake up) can make a huge difference. I have to admit that I'm terrible at doing this — the lure of my bed is often too strong — but when I do, I never regret it.
- If you have young children, create a visual chart of what needs to happen when. This can help everyone to get into the habit of getting ready on time, and also aids children in their independence, allowing them to see what needs to happen next.
- Get playful. For young children, it can be fun to time yourselves getting dressed each day, and try to beat your

personal best. See if the children can hop down the street to the car.

- Find ways to weave joy into your mornings. It might be creating a morning time rhythm (see next section) or simply setting the tone of the morning by playing beautiful — or fun — music, diffusing some essential oils, or all playing a game or doing a quiz over breakfast.

Morning time and tea time

Having a morning time or tea time rhythm can create a wonderful space for calm, injecting some connection into your day as you 'breathe in' together. The idea is simple: gathering together either in the morning over breakfast or in the afternoon over tea and a snack, and sharing pictures, books, music, board games, silly stories, discussion — in short, whatever you want to share which brings beauty and joy into your lives. Whether you gather twice a day or once a week, this coming together and sharing nourishment — both physical and mental — provides a welcome resetting and moment for connection. It can also be a wonderful way for you to weave what's important to you into your daily life, making time for meaningful moments to cherish, and it's a great place to start if you want to build a homeschooling rhythm into your days.

Morning time

Morning time can help mornings feel less rushed, more pleasant, calmer — starting the day off 'right' rather than hurrying to get out of the house. When home educating, some families like to keep a 'morning basket' close to the breakfast table with story books, art postcards, poetry, non-fiction reference books, paper and crayons, and anything else they'd like to share together. Some families enjoy using workbooks during this time too. If you have older children, this can be a great time to learn a few words of a foreign language, slowly work through a classic novel or play, or grapple with philosophical questions.

Tea time

Afternoon tea time can bring a welcome period of rest following an otherwise busy day, a pause to refuel and gather energy to get everyone through to the end of the day. A snack shared over a good book, board game, or documentary can again bring welcome connection, leaving everyone nourished and topped up before the evening routine of chores, supper, and bath time. And of course, tea time doesn't have to mean tea! But a good afternoon snack — for parents, too — can do wonders for everyone's mood heading into the evening.

Transitions

Transitions — moving from one activity to the next — can often be a tricky point for young children. Creating more predictability through rhythms can help children navigate transitions, because they learn to expect what is coming next so they aren't caught off-guard. When more rhythm is brought to these points, the whole day starts to flow better, with less conflict and stress all round.

With transitions, we need to lead by example. If you're

saying it's bedtime while you're still writing an email or washing up, your children will likely not want to stop playing. If you call your children to the table, the meal should be ready to eat — or perhaps they have been involved in cooking, or laying the table — and you should be ready to sit down and join them.

You could consider:

- Singing a simple song to mark transitions: 'We've had a lovely play, now it's time to tidy our toys away,' 'This is how we wash our hands, before we eat our breakfast,' or 'It's tea time, it's tea time, it's time to sit and have a snack.' It doesn't matter much which tune you use!

- Giving some warning when it is time to move onto the next thing so your child isn't caught unawares: 'After you have finished your game it will be time to wash our hands and go and have a sandwich for lunch,' or 'It is nearly time to leave the park. You have time to feed three more ducks, and then you can choose a stick to bring home.'

- Having a chart or drawing with all of the things which need to happen at certain times, and doing things in a certain order. You could laminate it, so that your child can tick things off as they go, and they might enjoy helping you decorate it. This also helps them to grow in independence as it's easier for them to learn the routine of what needs to get done.

The stronger your rhythm becomes, the easier transitions become to navigate because everyone knows what comes next.

Working space for self-care into your daily rhythm

As parents, getting enough time for self-care is important; not just for us, but for our families too. But finding the time can feel impossible, especially when navigating challenging periods.

To make time for more self-care in your daily life, you might want to:

Start small.

A few minutes to drink a cup of coffee before the children wake up. Listening to your favourite song or a podcast while you wash up. Breathing in the sound of the birds singing as you hang up the laundry. A chapter of your book while the baby naps. All of these things count as self-care in very different ways! Just carving out a few minutes here and there for yourself shows you that you are important too, and helps you to get your needs met.

Build some 'quiet time' into your daily rhythm.

After lunch works well, or when your children are napping, listening to an audiobook, or playing quietly. There may be some pushback from them at first when you say that you're not available to read or play for this time, but after a while it will become ingrained as just 'what we do', and everyone will benefit from you having half an hour to yourself.

Remember that self-care doesn't have to mean time away from your children!

Focusing on joyful activities you can do alongside your children which leave you feeling genuinely topped up is a brilliant way to take care of yourself when you don't get much time alone. Whether it's long walks in nature, watching a great film, a shared bubble bath, or curling up with a cup of tea on the sofa under a blanket while you read aloud to your child, find what it is you love doing together and make time for it.

I asked Grá Conway, an ex-teacher, now blogger and mother of two young children, why quiet time was such an important part of her family's daily rhythm:

'A daily quiet time is essential in our house, not only because my children are young enough to need a physical rest, but because it provides the mental and emotional rest from work and each other that we all need to enjoy our afternoon.

'During this time, we can process whatever emotions we have felt during the morning; if it's been fun-filled we can rest and recharge, and if it's been filled with tension then we can release it and let it go. I think modelling rest, relaxation, and reflection is crucial for children, especially nowadays when being busy is the norm.'

Weekly rhythms

Whether you usually work outside the home full-time, or you are with the children day in, day out, or something in between, crafting a weekly rhythm can bring a lot of security and predictability to young children, as well as creating mental space for you and ensuring you have time carved out for your own needs. A weekly rhythm allows your child to anticipate what will come next, and gives you freedom to plan your days knowing that you are living a life that has at least a hint of balance.

When crafting a weekly rhythm, you may want to think about:

- What needs to happen? (For example, work outside the home, homework or lessons, chores, any other commitments.)
- What would you like to happen? (For example, going for a run, trips to the park, playdates.) How can you balance this with what needs to happen?

Looking at the week as a whole allows you to see more clearly where you have space for more structure, or where there is too much already scheduled. It can also help you find more balance and ensure that, over the course of the week, everyone is getting their needs met, be those needs for physical exercise, time alone, or one-on-one time with parents.

If you are at home with your children, some gentle structure can really help your weeks feel more purposeful, with a predictable flow of days. Planning an activity each day — baking, a nature walk, an online art class, video-calling grandparents — can help to give shape to your weeks.

Rhythm is not just for children. Having an evening each

week to go to for a run or a date night with our partner each month (even if it's a takeaway pizza on the sofa in front of the TV) can make a huge difference to our lives, as we can anticipate that enjoyment and feel we have a right to it.

Sites of Mutual Fulfilment

The concept of Sites of Mutual Fulfilment was coined by New Zealand-based blogger, writer, and mother of two girls Lucy Aitkenread. I first came across it in 2016, and it's been influential in my work — and my own parenting — ever since.

Lucy writes:

'A Site of Mutual Fulfilment (SMF) is a place where both child and parent have a great time. It's pretty simple, but I think they should be one of the daily aims of every parent. If each day began with the question "Where is today's SMF?" we'd get to the end of the day without feeling utterly ragged. SMFs are different for every family. They are hidden everywhere. You can find them in the city, in the countryside. There are some in your own home even. Some are yet to be created by you and your friends ...

'A SMF is a place where both the child's and the parent's urges and needs are met. They are places where all parties leave with a full cup. They are the vital mental-health break in a day for mum or dad. Having enough SMFs planned throughout each week can make the difference in whether we enjoy parenting, or not.'

Sites of Mutual Fulfilment will look different for each family. I love gardening and baking with our daughter and feel genuinely refreshed and 'full' after doing so. My husband loves teaching her basic coding, and making dens where he can read aloud to her. As a family we love going into nature together for walks, but our favourite thing to do is have a playdate with another family where Frida gets on well with the other kids and we are friends with the parents (for me, it doesn't get much better than this). Perhaps your family's SMF is going bike riding, watching a movie together, going for a hike, or throwing a kitchen dance-party.

Making space in your weekly rhythm for some Sites of Mutual Fulfilment will increase your joy and connection, and make life feel easier and happier. Where possible, see if you can find ways to weave them in. It can be fun to make a list with your children and stick it up on the fridge, ready for those days that plans get unexpectedly cancelled or you're at a loose end.

When your weeks are unpredictable

When weeks are unpredictable, perhaps due to shift work or one parent working away, or other circumstances beyond your control, it's even more important to craft strong rhythms around key anchor points in the day: mornings, meals, bedtime. Even if bedtime switches between parents, grandparents, and a babysitter, keeping the rhythm consistent will allow your children to feel more secure and confident that they know what's happening to them.

It will help everyone if there is time for meaningful connection built into your rhythms. Although the actual time may vary from day to day, providing regular moments to release pressure — by reading, playing, telling stories, or having tickle fights — allows your children to reconnect with you and feel secure.

If a loved one is travelling or unavailable in person, build in regular video calls, allowing for a period of connection afterwards to help create a safe space for any strong feelings arising from speaking to the absent relative.

You could consider:

- Previewing the day to come at bedtime and again in the morning so your child has some sense of what will happen and there is transparency; they won't feel that they have been tricked! This is especially helpful if there is anything unusual about the day ('Tomorrow, Daddy will be having a fun day with you while I work'). This can even be useful for older children ('Your mum will be late home tomorrow so it would be great if you could start dinner for us').
- If there is uncertainty, be honest: 'Either I will pick you up or Dad will collect you. We aren't sure yet but whoever it is will come and meet you at the door.'
- Keeping some parts of the day and week consistent where you can: a candle at meal times, pasta on a Wednesday, or a family movie night on a Sunday.

Rhythm for differently wired children

Predictability and flow is important for all children. But for some neurodiverse children, it is even more vital to keeping them feeling safe and happy. ('Neurodiverse' is an umbrella term which can include children on the Autism spectrum, with Attention Deficit Hyperactivity Disorder, with Sensory Processing Disorders, or developmental delays.) Changes and transitions can feel especially hard for them, and rhythm may be more important than ever to them during periods of uncertainty. Unexpected events can result in 'emotional dysregulation'; outbursts of difficult feelings and behaviours that are very hard for them to control.

I spoke to Claire Chapple, who previously worked as a mental-health service manager and behavioural specialist before leaving to home educate her own neurodiverse daughter full time:

'Change is remarkably difficult for neurodiverse children, even where the smallest details are concerned. Even so, we can support them to adapt using highly regarded techniques. Visuals help children to process information where verbal communication is ineffective for the child; think calendars, visual routine steps, and "now, next, later" cards throughout each day.

'Sensory input such as "heavy work" [activities that provide a physical challenge and strong sensory feedback, for example digging or pulling a heavy wagon full of blocks] assists the dysregulated child to process the physical effects of anxiety due to change. But above all, honesty is the key to supporting neurodiverse children to adapt to change. Our children are seeing the changes, feeling the impact, and it's our responsibility as parents and caregivers to acknowledge the truth with them regarding the change, in a developmentally appropriate way.'

Rhythm when your child has two homes

What about if your child has two homes? Or what if you have step-children who stay with you some of the time? What might that rhythm look like? If your child shares their time between two homes, it's likely that you will already have built up a rhythm around this, with set times and dates to move from one home to the other. Here are a few ideas for bringing rhythm into homes where children may share their time:

- Keep times and days to move from one parent's home to the other predictable and consistent. Of course there might be times when things have to change at the last minute, but trying to keep a predictable pattern where possible can help children feel secure.
- Remind your child when they will be spending time with their other parent. This helps them anticipate the change and gives them an opportunity to plan ahead and get used to the idea of leaving.
- Create small rituals around the transition of leaving home to go to the other parent's home, and coming back to your home. Perhaps you always have a special snack together to reconnect, or you carefully pack a little note for your child to discover every time they leave, or your child's special toy always goes with them.
- Focus on the rhythm in your own home. It's all you can do. Of course, by all means have conversations with your co-parent about bedtime or meal time preferences, but remember that they will likely do things differently to you — and that's okay. Create your own anchors

and precious rituals to share together, and try to let go of any frustration if these rhythms aren't matched in your child's other home. 'In this home we ...' can be a useful phrase.

- Consider how things like phone or video calls with your child's other parent can also be woven into your child's rhythm — for example, every night before bed, or over breakfast on a Saturday. Again, aim to keep these consistent, for everyone's benefit.

Finding your rhythm when working from home

This may not be what you want to hear, but I feel like I need to say it anyway: working from home with children around — especially young children — is hard. It is quite simply impossible to give both your attention full-time, and the guilt which can come from feeling like neither your job nor your kids are getting the best of you is real.

However, many parents don't have any choice but to balance the two. Perhaps you usually work outside the home, but aren't able to at the moment; maybe you run your own business around the children while home educating; or you've come to a deal with your boss where you can work flexible hours around caring for your children.

Rhythm can be especially helpful if you have to work from home around your children, whether long- or short-term. But what that rhythm looks like can vary hugely from family to family.

Balancing working and childcare

I wanted to get advice from someone who is experienced in working from home around children, so I spoke to Annie Ridout, a mother of three young children and author of *The Freelance Mum* and the upcoming book *Shy*, who said:

'I used the sleepy newborn months, when the babies were immobile, to do short bursts of work. If I had the energy, and the ideas, I enjoyed focusing my mind on something other than nappies and sleep (or lack thereof). But I didn't put any pressure on myself. If I achieved something other than looking after my newborn, great. If not — no big deal. New motherhood is challenging enough already. Working with a newborn was harder when I had my second baby, as I then had a toddler, and harder still when I had my third. But TV meant the older kid(s) could be entertained for at least 20 minutes, so while the baby breastfed or slept, I could tap out some words on my iPhone.'

Annie, who also runs online courses for freelancers and entrepreneurs, continued:

'I have learned to be productive in tiny pockets of time, as I have never had the luxury of full-time childcare. It's the same for most freelance mums, I think. We feel that because we are at home, we should only have part-time childcare for the kids (or none at all). But what then happens is that we work evenings and weekends and burn out. So I always advise that self-employed parents do invest in as much childcare as they can, from when it feels right. I now have three kids aged five, three, and seven months. My husband and I work together, from home, running online courses — so we are in a nice position in terms of sharing all roles:

childcare, housework, earning money. But it can also be hard to separate work and "life". We try, therefore, to keep work (for us) and learning (for the kids) to weekdays, and weekends are for play, dancing, and films.'

I asked Annie what tips she would give parents who are juggling working from home — perhaps unexpectedly — while they have children at home, and she said:

'Lower your expectations about what's possible and do the minimum. Always have a realistic "to-do" list for that day. That might be "write one Instagram post"; it might be "create an online course". We all have different allotted work times, and work at difference paces. On that note, don't worry about what other people are doing. Work in a way that suits you and your family. Celebrate every success; it's so important to focus on the things that are going right. And think creatively about what you can do, when. I often write an Instagram post while breastfeeding the baby before he goes to bed. It's a long, sleepy feed and just enough time to create a post.'

Although working from home around children can be challenging, especially if they are young, there are things you can do to give yourself the best chance. Here are some further tips from me:

Create a working rhythm.

First, get clear on what is non-negotiable. What has to happen, and when? Do you have a weekly conference call you need to attend? Do you have certain deadlines? Are there times you need to be in front of your computer?

What about your children — what anchors can you keep fixed in your days and weeks where you will be able to give them your time and attention? Then sit down and see if you can break these down into chunks of time when you can work, ideally keeping some bigger stretches aside for when you need to work uninterrupted, as well as shorter bursts for answering emails and ticking smaller jobs off your to-do list. You might need to play around with your rhythm at first to find something that works for you; remember, rhythm is meant to be flexible!

Get creative about when you work.

Communicate honestly with your partner; if you live in a two-parent household, find time to discuss your workload with one another each week, going through any deadlines or big projects you have coming up. Create a weekly plan where you mark down any important calls or virtual meetings, and try to arrange these so that the other parent can be available to the children (or if this isn't possible, this could be a good time to put a film on — see below). Can one of you work early mornings, and the other work evenings? Who might be able to work at the weekend? Could anyone work compressed hours, or a nine-day fortnight where alternate Fridays are taken off? Is there any leeway around lunchtimes? Many of my clients have found creative ways to balance working from home around looking after their children by making compromises like the ones I've just described. Sometimes these compromises don't feel ideal — my husband and I have had to navigate periods where weekends and evenings simply don't exist in the traditional sense, as we manage busy workloads with homeschooling our daughter — but they can be the difference between making it work and not.

If possible, invite your children to work alongside you from time to time.

For a toddler or pre-schooler, this might mean short bursts of drawing, painting, or working on a puzzle before they go off to play; an older child or teenager might enjoy doing schoolwork, writing a letter, or working on a project alongside you. You could even set up side-by-side 'work spaces'.

Use screen-time to your advantage.

Build in one or two regular times for TV or gaming each day. (I've found late afternoons when energy is flagging can work really well.) Not only does this all but guarantee you some quiet time to make any calls you need to make, or undertake work tasks which need silence, but having a set time for screens can reduce conflict and arguments about when it's time to watch TV, too. As well as watching films or shows, this might be a time when children take an online class, do a fun exercise video, or video-call friends or family.

Prioritise your work tasks ruthlessly.

Consider not checking emails until you've done the three most urgent things from your list, or removing anything which has gone un-actioned for more than a fortnight. Also, it helps to be clear with your clients or employer about what you can and can't deliver. Boundaries around your time can feel uncomfortable to establish, but in the long run they will benefit everyone.

Ask for support.

If you usually work from home, see if another parent you know might be up for playdate swaps. If you can afford some childcare (even if you are home educating — many homeschooling families work and use some childminders, babysitters, clubs, or nurseries), then even a few hours can be incredibly useful to guarantee a solid stretch of work. If this is not possible, or you find yourself working from home at short notice, please don't feel guilty if the TV is on all afternoon so that you can finish off a big project. Do what you have to do to make it work.

Be kind to yourself.

Working from home with young children around is so hard, and there will be days when you just can't keep on top of work, or where you've barely seen the kids. Sometimes just getting through the day will be enough.

Breathing in, breathing out — again

The 'breathe in, breathe out' pattern is especially useful to ensure that you're giving your children the connection and presence they need — and if they are young, they will need a lot — to give yourself the best chance at getting your work done in those breathe-out periods. If you can, put any distractions away during the time you've marked out to really be with your children, whether you're sharing a meal, reading, playing, or cooking together. You will find they will be far more willing to then play or work alongside you if you've been able to give them some focused attention first.

Adapting to your new normal

While it might take you and your children a little while to find a flow that works, keep going. Some days will inevitably be harder than others; some days your children will be sick, or sad, or will simply need you more than usual. Some days you will have deadlines that make you feel impatient, stressed, and frustrated. Allowing everyone some grace and remembering that no one is expecting you to be a perfect parent can really help. If a day needs to be a complete write-off, there's always tomorrow.

What about weekends?

Weekends can feel loaded with expectation and pressure at the best of times. It's easy to want your precious time spent as a family to be perfect — it certainly looks like everyone else's is, on social media! — yet it's all too easy to end each weekend feeling like there hasn't been enough time to get everything done, spending each Sunday night feeling disappointed that you didn't spend enough time with the children, or that the kitchen is still messy, or that you once again didn't manage to go for the run you've been trying to go on for months.

It's easy to want to say yes to everything at weekends — birthday parties, playdates, classes, and special outings — but this can lead to feeling frazzled and exhausted at the end of it. When you say yes to something, you are always saying no to something else.

If you said no more, what could you be saying yes to instead? More rest? More connection as a family?

Weekends can also sometimes highlight a mismatch between the expectations of the different family members who share a home. Do you have a shared vision for how you'd like to spend your precious weekend time, or do you all have different ideas of things you really want to do?

It can be helpful to create a weekend rhythm, with lots of free space for changing needs and desires, but enough structure that your weekends don't float past, leaving you wondering where they went. It might be pancakes on a Saturday, or pencilling in half an hour of downtime to read the papers while the children play, ensuring you've left enough time to video-call your relatives, or making sure that you're out of the house by ten o'clock on a Saturday morning for an adventure — whatever works for your family.

Weekends in times of change

In times of change — from crises to school holidays — weekends might take on a different meaning. If the children aren't in childcare or school, and no one is going into work, weekends and weekdays might feel like they are melting into one. This is where keeping up some of those small rituals can help bring a sense of normality and security, no matter what else is going on around you.

Seasonal rhythms

The summer watermelons, the winter soups. Seasonal rhythms help children feel connected to the cyclical nature of time and the passing of the seasons, the changing seasons providing a revitalising but reassuring rhythm of their own. Tapping into that seasonal cycle can serve as a wonderful basis for family connection and creativity, even when life as you usually know it looks different to usual.

Crafting seasonal rhythms is an easy way to bring more of what you value into your family life. Togetherness is fostered in shared celebrations, both as a family and in the wider community. Activities repeated throughout the seasons, year after year, slowly become woven into the fabric of family life. Handmade Valentine's Day cards. Spring cleaning. Growing sunflowers each year. Back-to-school supply shopping. New slippers each autumn. Growing pine-cone collections. These small actions, repeated lovingly year after year, become part of 'what we do' — the moments our children will look back on when grown, and perhaps recreate with their own children.

Birthdays are probably the ultimate family celebration. Children feel so much anticipation around them, parents often feel keenly the emotions of passing time, and everyone gathers in joy to celebrate a beloved member of the family. Creating family rhythms and traditions around birthdays is a wonderful way to introduce more rhythm to the home and increase anticipation, while reducing overwhelm for everyone.

Marking the seasons and seasonal festivals throughout the year adds so much to family life. The joy is not just in the celebrating, but in the preparation for these celebrations and rituals. They do not have to be elaborate, expensive, or time-consuming. You could consider:

- Having certain activities you do each season: planting seeds in spring — in a window box, if you don't have a garden, a trip to the beach in summer, carving pumpkins in autumn, candle-lit breakfasts in winter.
- Creating a list of ideas at the beginning of each season and sticking this up on the fridge. 'Collect autumn leaves', 'Make a map of local trees with pretty blossoms', 'Find the biggest seashell we can'. This can be brilliantly helpful if you're at a loss for things to do.
- Reading seasonal books, putting away the old and bringing out the new at the beginning of each new season. (We've been doing this since our daughter was tiny and it's so lovely to rediscover old favourites year after year.)
- Celebrating the equinoxes with a simple meal and a small gift or a new book.
- Creating traditions around any festivals you celebrate. Maybe you always bake gingerbread at Christmas, decorate the house for Eid, or pick your own apples for Rosh Hashanah.
- Changing your meal rhythm each season to reflect local weather and produce, perhaps bringing out a candle for the winter months, or adding a cheap bunch of daffodils

to the table in the spring.

- Building nature walks into your weekly rhythm to observe the changes in the local wildlife.
- Setting up a nature table (this can be a windowsill, corner of a desk, or basket), which slowly changes following the seasonal shifts.
- Using the seasonal changes as a time to clean the home, sort through clothing to make sure everything still fits, and do a gentle declutter of your spaces.
- Looking at the moon together each night to learn its phases.

Creating a visual rhythm

Young children love having visuals to refer to, so you might like to make a visual rhythm chart for your days, weeks, or other part of your day, such as bedtime.

Keep these simple. If your days and weeks change a lot, you could consider making a laminated chart with different images to blu-tack on each Sunday evening. A visual rhythm is not meant to be a routine to stick to religiously. Sometimes you will deviate from it because, well, that's life. But having a visual reminder can help everyone learn what comes next, providing anticipation for the fun and time to prepare for the not-so-fun.

The process of sitting down and visually planning out your days or weeks is also a great way of seeing if you have achieved the balance you are aiming for. You can add meals to each day if you have decided to implement a meal rhythm, or chores such as grocery shopping or mopping the floors, but keep them relatively simple — less is more (and is easier to stick to, too).

Suggestions for visual rhythms

There are many kinds of visual rhythm that you could choose from, so feel free to experiment with what works best for your family. Here are some you might like to consider:

- Basic 'tick chart'. This works well for mornings, evenings, or any times that a set number of things needs to happen (useful for getting out of the house!).
- Daily rhythm chart. These work well if your daily rhythm is consistent. For example, breakfast, getting dressed, going outside, structured learning time, lunch, quiet time, playtime, snack, art, supper, bath, bed. If the rhythm of your days varies, you could create removable pictures with velcro or blu-tack so you can update the chart each morning to reflect the day's plans.
- Weekly rhythm chart. These work well if your weekly rhythm is quite consistent. You can also pair these with figures or markers to clearly show the day of the week, which works well for young children. You could add a meal to each day of the week too.
- Seasonal chart or rhythm wheel. This is a nice way to visually show where you are in the year, highlighting the cyclical nature of the seasons. These can work well when used in conjunction with other charts too, as you change them less frequently (say, on the first of each

month) so it's not overwhelming. You can also add special days like Christmas, birthdays, etc.

There are lots more ideas on social media and Pinterest if you're looking for inspiration.

Reclaiming your rhythm when life throws you a curve-ball

Some seasons in life are harder or less predictable than others. Sometimes these periods are relatively short: an illness which knocks you for a week, a period of disruption when you change to a new job or your children move childcare or school. Sometimes these periods of change feel longer: a new baby in the family and all of the adjustments and feelings which come with them; the grief of losing a loved one or a long period of family illness; adjusting to a parent working away from home (or quitting work outside the home altogether to stay at home); separating from a partner; enforced isolation due to a global health crisis; unexpected disruption from flooding or hurricanes. Change can be hard on everyone.

Focusing on keeping strong anchors of predictability throughout the day and week — meal time rhythms, bedtime rhythms, snuggling up first thing in the morning, Saturday pancakes, Sunday bike rides — allows everyone to feel calmer and more secure when other parts of your life are changing.

Even when your rhythms are well established and life feels calm, you can find that they need reclaiming or adjusting.

Children drop naps. Bedtimes shift with the seasons. Time outdoors becomes harder during extremes of temperature. Maybe something that was working well no longer fits everyone's needs, or a change in your life means that things can't carry on as they were before.

Having a family rhythm doesn't prevent the hard times from happening; sometimes life will stray from the dreams we have for our family. But it can make times of change and adjustment easier, your rhythms bringing comfort and predictability to times when the world feels as though it is shifting under your feet.

Rhythm in the Home summary

- Rhythm is different to routine. Rather than a strict schedule where things are planned to the minute, it is a predictable flow built on daily anchors and rituals.
- Establishing a strong rhythm can take time, but in times of uncertainty more than ever it is the best way to bring a feeling of security and calm to your daily life.
- Build your daily rhythms around predictable anchors: meal times, mornings, and bedtimes, and then go from there. You could add in small rituals, too: a candle at meal times, a family walk after lunch.
- Seasonal rhythms help children feel connected to the cyclical nature of time and the passing of the seasons. Tapping into that seasonal cycle can serve as a wonderful basis for family connection and creativity, even when life looks different to usual.
- Rhythm can be especially important when working from home. Finding times to connect with your children between calls and emails helps everyone to stay happy, and you can relax knowing you have dedicated work times when you can really focus.
- Creating visual rhythm charts can help younger children see the pattern of the day and learn what is expected from them.

Chapter Three

Toys, play, and the prepared environment

Our homes matter. They are the stage for the most intimate theatre of family life: the claps as the baby takes her first steps, the arguments over stepped-upon LEGO, the perfect moments snuggled up in bed together as a family, the homework at the kitchen table while dinner cooks, the hugs following the first teary heartbreak. Far from being superficial, our home environments have the power to create calm or incite conflict, to promote deep play and study, or lead to cries of, 'I don't have any toys.' And in those moments when you and your family are spending more time at home, your space matters more than ever before.

The home as a 'prepared environment'

The 'prepared environment' is an idea which comes from influential Italian educator Maria Montessori. Montessori believed that a child's environment can be designed to facil-itate maximum independent learning and exploration. The prepared environment refers to a space — such as a classroom or home — which has been designed with children in mind, and which has the goal of giving them as much independence as possible. The six principles of the prepared environment are: freedom, structure and order, beauty, nature and reality, social environment, and intellectual environment.

This idea of the prepared environment has been pivotal to how I have approached curating our family home, and it's something I think every parent can be inspired by, even if they are unfamiliar with the rest of Montessori's work.

You do not need a lot of money or fancy equipment to create a space that encourages learning, connection, and play. In fact, by the end of this chapter, you might have decided against buying anything at all, instead preferring to get rid of things which are cluttering what would otherwise be a great environment. This approach will work everywhere, from a four-bedroom house to a one-bedroom apartment.

The prepared environment will look different in each home, reflecting the family's individual needs, culture, resources, and style, and the children's stages of development. However, prepared environments will usually have some things in common:

- They are calm and orderly — at least some of the time! (Young children don't always make this their priority.)
- They are set up to help children succeed in doing things independently.
- They understand that when it comes to toys and materials, less is more; though you don't need to be minimalist to do Montessori, keeping a space simple helps reduce overwhelm and visual clutter.
- They make space for beauty, be it through flowers, art, or cultural objects.

The prepared environment is not perfect. It gets messy, things get spilled, muddy footprints get made. But it is intentional, thoughtful, and based on your family's unique needs, and it is these qualities which can turn your home into a space where your children thrive.

Think cosy, not classroom

When children are young, their brains are like sponges, soaking up everything around them. It stands to reason that, just as they soak up language, facial expressions, music, and manners, children soak up their environments, too — and it follows that we would want to create a tranquil, inviting, and beautiful space for them to spend time in. I don't think this is shallow; the spaces we regularly spend time in have an impact on how we feel and our quality of life. As Montessori said, 'The things [the child] sees are not just remembered; they form a part of his soul.' Our spaces have an impact on us; coming home to a cluttered house or apartment makes most people feel stressed, whereas having clear, organised spaces can help us feel calmer and more in control.

Think about your dream home environment. Your child's is probably not very different! There is often a perceived need for children's spaces to be brightly coloured and packed with toys and materials, but this can be overwhelming and over-stimulating for them as well as us.

A 2015 study by Barrett et al. on the impact of classroom design on pupils' learning found that the aesthetics of classrooms actually have a significant impact on children's ability to take in information. Classrooms that have too much colour and too many display items were found to have a negative effect on learning outcomes, distracting children and making it harder for them to focus, while classrooms with no decor or display items at all were also correlated with lower learning outcomes. Natural light and fresh air were the most important ingredients for happy, focused pupils, as well as furniture which fits the children's needs, and the flexibility to move the space around.

Forget trying to turn your home into a classroom; instead, what the research shows us is that classrooms should be more like homes! Natural light, fresh air, flexibility, and a sense of homeliness through carefully considered decoration (but without filling every available space with charts and posters) are all things you can offer your children, no matter the size of your home. I'd go as far as saying that if you're homeschooling, one of your biggest educational assets is your home. As we'll see in Chapter Four, children don't learn well when stressed. Turning your home into a place where your children feel empowered and relaxed is one of the best things you can do to help them thrive.

Making space for beauty

Some things you could consider:

Spring clean — at any time of year.
   Throw open the windows, air out cupboards and duvets, deep-clean the bathroom and kitchen, and give any

scuffed or grubby walls a coat of fresh paint. If you rent your home, check with your landlord first, but some will be happy for you to paint walls as long as you paint any bright colours back to neutral before you move out. Make sure you've got any products you need to clean with — simple items like a basic cleaning spray, some cloths, a broom, and a mop are fine — you're aiming for the space to be reasonably clean, not immaculate.

Tips on cleaning for people who hate to clean

I spoke to Hannah Bullivant, an interiors and events stylist and mother of two children, who shared these tips on cleaning for people who hate to clean:

- 'Tidy up first. Clearing surfaces makes it so much quicker to clean. Chuck out any unwanted junk, properly sort paperwork (don't just straighten the pile or move it around!), put toys and kid stuff back in its place, and recycle magazines.
- 'Use lovely cleaning tools. I have slowly been upgrading my cleaning tools over the last few years, and it has helped me to rethink how I approach cleaning and housework. I have found that everyday life is a little more pleasurable when the mundane objects you encounter every day are beautiful. When you have to sweep up crushed food stuffs of unidentifiable age from the floor, the frustration is somewhat countered by using a brush and crumb tray that looks and feels good to use.
- 'Listen to podcasts or really good music. This really makes a difference to my resentment levels when I need

to clean! Podcasts in particular have the added benefit of teaching me something new while I'm cleaning or
tidying, and this somehow makes all the difference in
how long it feels like it takes.

- 'Use lovely scented products. The other thing which I
think makes a difference is to use products that smell
good and aren't full of chemicals. I make my own products, which means I can scent them how I want; it's
much cheaper, and comes with a sense of extra satisfaction when one does finally tackle the mountainous
washing basket.

- 'Do it with others! I much prefer cleaning if my husband
is doing it too — firstly because I believe in shared domestic labour, but also because it's more enjoyable to
do chores with someone you like! Similarly, if I'm able
to get the kids involved, it's much quicker and more fun
too. We can sometimes get them involved by letting
them choose a "tidy-up song" to play really loud.'

Think about the small touches you can add.

A child-sized table and chair (IKEA does a great, very
affordable, set) with a small vase, a jar of crayons, and some
paper. An art print taped at child height. A plant to care
for. Nature finds, displayed on a shelf or in a basket. Fresh
flowers or branches responsibly foraged from a local green
space. String hung up from wall to wall to hang paintings
on. Music playing softly in the background. Gentle
lighting; fairy lights and candles can do a lot to brighten
up grey days. Soft rugs or blankets to cuddle up with a
pile of books. All of these things add beauty and comfort,

and encourage your child to relax and feel calm, and learn effectively whether you are home educating or not. Not everyone lives in a big home with a playroom, vegetable patch, and mud kitchen, but you can still get creative when it comes to how you use your space; our dining area doubles up as a homeschooling space, and our living area doubles up as a playroom. I know families who homeschool at the kitchen table, or on the sofa, and families who have created a 'family bedroom' and used a second bedroom to create a separate play space. If you can't accommodate a separate child-sized table and chair, perhaps you could create a reading corner with some books, cushions, and pictures at child height; whatever the size of the space you live in and whatever the layout, rest assured that your space can invite and entice your children to play, learn, and rest.

Making smaller spaces work for you

I spoke to Africa Daley-Clarke, who lives in a two-bedroom flat in London with her husband and two daughters:

'My top tip for making smaller spaces work for you is curating with intention. Before starting on a room, my husband and I brainstorm all the things we'd like and need from the space. These don't need to be just practical items; we include our "wish list" items too. Once we've got a comprehensive list down for the family, we create a really basic, but to-scale, drawing, and play around with layout; often it's at this stage I realise some of my ideas aren't practical. We're no strangers to second-hand and selling our old pieces, so that always helps in raising the funds for the next piece. We've always been happy to wait some time for the perfect item rather than rush and buy the first thing we see, and because we truly believe building the home you love should take time, we find a real joy in finding what we need slowly.'

Africa, who is expecting her third child, continued:

'Despite living in a modest two-bedroom flat, we have tried to make sure that every single room apart from our bedroom is functional and accessible for the children as well as us. Toys may have a dedicated space in their bedroom, but each room space remains child friendly and we try not to be too precious about anything, remembering this is their home just as much as ours.'

Gentle decluttering.

Get rid of broken toys, donate clothes which no longer fit, sort through piles of drawings in the corners of the room, and try to find everything a home. This can feel like an overwhelming project, especially if you have young children and time is at a premium, but it can save lots of time and energy in the long run. I've found that when things all have a space, tidying up takes less time and feels less daunting. Start with one small task — a kitchen drawer, or the entrance to your home where bags and shoes can pile up — and you'll soon notice the difference.

Your home is for living, not a show home

It's important to stress, however, that even a carefully considered home environment does not mean things are going to be spotless. Kids tend to create mess, and if you're in a season of your life where you're home more than usual — perhaps due to a new baby, a cold winter or heatwave, an unforeseen crisis, or if you're homeschooling — then a certain level of mess comes with the territory. It feels impossible, but try not to compare yourself to what you see in magazines or on social media. As my husband said to me once, 'Our house looks much nicer on Instagram.' (Thanks Sam!) But his point is valid: I rarely share the dusty corners, the laundry piles, or the mouldy tomato I found at the back of the fridge on social media. It's a cliché, but comparing yourself to these kinds of images really is comparing your reality to someone's carefully curated highlights reel.

Yes, our homes matter: they have the ability to make people feel welcome or uneasy, to invite creativity or to stifle it. But just because you're now thinking carefully about your prepared environment and what might go into your space, it doesn't mean it's the time to buy a fancy new sofa or put down cream carpet! One of our sofas is on its last legs after being jumped and climbed on for five years, but I'm loath to replace it because that freedom to say yes to Frida jumping on it is important to me; I'd rather have old furniture and scruffy floors for a few years than spend my days stressed out or restricting her play because they might get damaged.

The best space for you won't necessarily be what works well on Pinterest, but a home which meets your family's needs.

Adapting your home to different life stages

I spoke to Jasmine Chong, a Singaporean teacher who has trained in both traditional and Montessori education, as well as in interior design. Jasmine is a parent educator and mother of two children, and she had this to say on creating a thoughtful home environment:

'Every stage of life is beautiful in its own right. Design for your now, rather than what you wish your home or life to be. If you have a toddler, embrace the mess and spills as a badge of real family life, and develop systems for sanity (for us, designating a place for everything, and everything in its place means that order can be restored fairly smoothly). If you tend towards organised clutter and bright colours, lean into that instead of trying in vain to empty your house of colour, personality, and sentimental items.

Jasmine, who also runs the popular blog *Three Minute Montessori*, continued:

'Keep your eyes peeled for unexpected treasures with serious learning potential when you travel or go thrifting; it isn't always the brand-name toys that children remember, but the oddities: the vintage puzzle, the flea-market porcelain teacups that they served flower tea in, the carved wooden animal from the southeast Asian market that somehow fits with the rest of their figurines.

'Know, too, that your home environment is never really "final"; it will grow and evolve in many iterations along with your child, unlike a classroom where the materials are by and large fixed. And if the environment doesn't invite activity, exploration, or curiosity, then we always look at how we can fix the environment, not the child. Because children are so attuned to the tiniest details, a small change, like adding a tiny bud vase with a single flower, or clearing the desk, can work wonders in renewing their interest in their environment.'

Meeting your family's needs through your home

What is important to you as a family? If you wrote down your family's needs and values in the last chapter, go back and remind yourself what they were. Then take a look around you. Are your family's needs being served through your home environment?

Taking the time to think about your home in this way can feel like a luxury. But many of my clients have found that just by making some small changes to their home layout, their relationship with their children has felt easier and calmer, and they have experienced less challenging behaviour and fewer conflicts.

Creating a 'yes space'

By carefully preparing your home environment, you create a 'yes space': one where your children are free — and, crucially, are safe — to touch, explore, move, climb, and look after their own needs. Creating 'yes spaces' in your home allows everyone to feel more relaxed; you feel more at ease knowing they are unlikely to do serious damage to anything, and your children feel less frustrated.

This means creating a space which is safe. This may include:

- Getting on your child's level. This might mean lying on the floor or getting on your hands and knees. What can you see?
- Putting locks on cupboards with cleaning products, not having heavy objects at a height where they could be pulled down, and keeping wires tidy under furniture where they are harder to reach.
- Making one room the 'safe' room to begin with. This can be especially helpful with an older baby or younger toddler. If you start with one room, I would still encourage you to look at making the whole of your home as child-friendly as possible.
- Ensuring your young child has ample opportunities to practise gross motor activities, such as climbing, in an appropriate way. This could be as simple as creating cushion mountains to climb over, or obstacle courses with chairs and tables.
- Teaching, rather than hiding away or saying no. Crockery and cutlery are a good example of this, but it can also apply to things like allowing your child to learn to safely climb onto a chair rather than telling them no, keeping stairs un-gated, or showing your young child how to gently handle and water a pot plant rather than moving it onto a high shelf.

I love that 'yes spaces' effectively negate the need for a lot of traditional discipline. If you don't have any breakable ornaments low down, you don't need to tell your children not to touch them; if the sofa is able to be jumped on, you no longer need to have arguments about not jumping on it. Having a space where you can say yes instead of no goes a long way towards building a family environment which feels easy, relaxed, and joyful.

What your space looks like will, of course, depend on your home and your family, as well as your tolerance for risk and the amount of time you have available to supervise your young children — for example, it might work not to have a stairgate with one child, but with three young children you may decide it's easier to have one.

How to cultivate a prepared environment if you move around a lot

I spoke to Dr Leighton Thomas, an education expert and home-educating mother to two young boys, about how she balances frequent work-related home moves with creating a space which feels calm and secure for her sons: 'Navigating frequent moves often means multiple stints in temporary housing situations too. When life looks and feels so different, we strive for a balance between re-creating home and treating each temporary space and location as its own unique adventure. We lean into relational connection, a few points of daily consistency (e.g. rhythms tied to sleeping and waking), curiosity for the fun we can discover, and a heaps of grace for everyone.

'Practically, a prepared environment helps too. Our luggage always includes a folding stool, a set of child-sized dishes and cutlery, a few jute baskets to hold toys or socks, and removable wall hooks for hanging coats or towels.'

Meeting your child's need for independence

One of the fundamental aspects of the prepared environment — whether it's in the classroom or in your home — is that it supports children to be independent through thoughtful planning and design. This is something that everyone can do in their homes, no matter the size or budget, and you may be surprised by the huge difference it makes, adding more ease into your daily life as your children begin to do things by themselves more frequently.

To encourage and enable your child's desire for independence in the home, you could:

- Have a clear space for your baby to practise moving and crawling around independently.
- Have low, sturdy furniture or a pull-up bar for your infant to pull themselves up on.
- Organise a small wardrobe or dresser so your child can select their own clothing from a few simple options.
- Place a mirror low down so your young child can observe themselves and care for themselves, brushing hair or washing faces.
- Have child-size furniture that your toddler can get in and out of by themselves, such as an adaptable high chair or floor-bed.
- Keep toys and materials in shallow baskets or low shelves and books in low, open-faced bookshelves so your child

can find what they want to play with, and later learn to put toys and books back in their proper place.

- Create a small snack station: a few crackers in an easy to open container and a piece of fruit is fine to start with.
- Give older children free access to scissors, knives, and other tools they may need.
- Provide access to water with a water dispenser for a child who can't yet easily use the sink.
- Put step-stools at various points in your home, such as by sinks and the kitchen counter, so your child can be involved in self-care and cooking.

When children are given the tools and space they need to be independent, it can diminish frustration and conflict for the whole family. Children don't need to ask for help all the time, are treated as the capable people they are, and are able to feel like useful members of the household. And I don't know about you, but I feel like reducing the number of times I'm asked to fetch my daughter water or a snack, and being genuinely helped when it comes to chores or prepping dinner are pretty excellent bonuses too.

Meeting your child's need to create

Having a dedicated space in your home for arts, crafts, projects, and 'table work' not only contains the mess that is inevitably created when kids get creative, but helps children know where all of their supplies are kept (and enables them to tidy up after themselves). Whether you have a whole room in your home to dedicate to art materials, or you only have space for a basket with a few materials which can be carried to a table, there are many ways to create an art space. Wall-hung spice racks, shelves, and pegboards can all hold art materials and free up valuable floor space (or protect art materials from tiny fingers if you have a baby or toddler around). An 'art cart' can be moved to the place where your child is working and keep all the materials in one place. Coffee tables can be covered in newspaper to create an impromptu art station.

In your art space, you might consider including:

- Art materials: coloured and plain paper, card, notebooks, scissors, coloured pencils, wax crayons, solid and liquid watercolour paints, washable paints, felt-tip markers, stickers, highlighters, oil pastels, Washi tape, glue, hole punch, stapler (depending on age), fine liners, stamps, and stencils are all great to have to hand. We have built up a collection of art materials over many holidays and birthdays!
- Recycling — toilet rolls, cereal boxes — for junk modelling, and old catalogues and magazines for collages.
- An apron for your child to wear. (I love aprons which have velcro side fastenings so that young children can put them on independently.)
- A floor mat. This is a must if your art space is in a room which has flooring that can't be easily washed. You can use an old rug if you don't have a mat.
- Old newspapers or an oilcloth to protect your table, if your child will be working at a multi-purpose table, e.g. the dining table.

- Big rolls of paper or an easel. You could also paint a blackboard wall — this can then be painted over when you move out if you're renting.
- A space for your child to display their own work if they wish to: string across the ceiling, a pinboard, or a big empty frame all work well to display (and contain!) work.
- Books about art and artists to look at for inspiration.
- Easy access to water for painting and washing up.
- Older children might also like access to a camera, printer, glue gun, and other equipment.

Giving your child free access to art materials can feel a little daunting at first — what about the mess, I hear you cry! — so if it's making you feel anxious, start small with something like a tin of crayons and some plain paper. Children are always going to want to experiment with art materials; it's just part of exploring the world. But if you teach them at a young age how to use materials correctly, it will buy you a lot more time when they are older of not having to hover over them every time they pull out the paints.

Meeting your child's need for movement

For children, the distinction between learning and movement doesn't really exist. Children need to move their bodies regularly, and movement is a key factor in how they integrate their social and academic learning and transform it into memory (Mualem at al., 2018). Freely chosen and directed, physically active play is crucially important for children's development in all areas of their lives. This means that when families have to spend more time at home, and perhaps aren't able to visit parks, pools, or trails, it can feel hard to find ways for children to get their need for movement met. But even if you live in a small space, there are things you can do to maximise your child's ability to move their bodies:

- Set up a laptop or TV with a clear space to move for your child to participate in virtual yoga, dance, or other sports classes.
- Push furniture to the side of the room so that your children have space to dance around.
- Take brain breaks every hour where you run round the block, or do twenty jumping jacks, or ten push-ups.
- Create obstacle courses with furniture, sofa cushions, upturned kitchen pans, and wooden planks.
- If you have a space where it would work, consider installing a bar or gymnastics rings over the door for the children to hang on, an indoor swing, a mini trampoline, or a climbing wall with a crash pad underneath. I've even seen some families ditch the sofa altogether, favouring indoor play-gym equipment with monkey bars and climbing accessories, or even indoor slides. I love this, as it shows they've really thought about their family's needs — but don't worry if it's not for you!
- If you have an outdoor space, think about installing a climbing frame, swing, slide, or trampoline. You could also add big logs for climbing and balancing, and branches or sticks for den making.

Meeting your child's need for rest

I think many parents spend a lot of time considering how to meet their children's need for movement; so many of my clients say about their children, 'They just have so much energy.' And, of course, as we have just been exploring, children do have a very real need to move their bodies throughout the day. But something I hear parents talking about less is how to support their children in getting enough rest throughout the day to balance those moments of energetic play. Yet rest is important. It allows our bodies to heal when we are unwell, and gives our brains the chance to process and consolidate information.

Here are some ways you can encourage rest in your home:

- Keep a pile of blankets and books on the sofa to encourage snuggling up together.
- Create a cosy corner for your children to unwind in, with a yoga mat, cushions, and some soft toys: perfect for having daily quiet time for children who no longer nap.
- During quiet time, play calm music, burn essential oils or candles that smell nice, turn on the soft lighting, and turn off the TV or radio and instead switch on an audiobook.
- Keep bedrooms feeling calm, where possible. If you have space for toys in other rooms, then keep children's bedrooms predominantly as a space for rest, with just a few books and toys, but if that's the only space to keep toys, you could consider keeping them covered at night with a few cloths or scarves over baskets.

- Model rest yourself! Let your children see you sit down, put your feet up, and pick up a book every so often. Take baths when you can. Create your own cosy spot or invitation to rest by piling up snacks, great books, headphones, a notebook, and blankets next to your bed or sofa. Prioritise your own need to rest when the baby is napping rather than jumping up to do chores. (We'll talk about this more in Chapter Five.)

Modern society can feel relentless, full of pressure to do more! Better! Faster! A full diary is seen in many circles as the ultimate affirmation of worth. And children are not immune from this pressure, with playdates, sports clubs, tutoring, and classes filling the 'free' time around school. Within this context, prioritising rest — for the whole family — can feel radical.

Meeting your child's need for play

One of the things I'm proudest of when it comes to our home — apart from the number of plants and books I've worked hard to cram into a relatively small space — is that the children we know all love coming over to play. I could tell myself it's because of my brilliant hosting skills and my willingness to bake cakes at a moment's notice, but really it's because our home is well set up for children to step through the front door and immediately get to down to the important work of play.

Play is vital for a happy, healthy childhood. It's the most important thing children can do — with Montessori calling it 'the work of childhood' — leading to a whole raft of academic, physical, social, and emotional benefits. Children of all ages have an urgent need for unstructured time where they are able to freely follow their own ideas and interests, explore what they want to explore, and act and move in ways they want to act and move. And yet in many countries around the world, the amount of time school-age children get to play each day is drastically declining, with a 2007 study from the American Academy of Pediatrics finding that 'despite the benefits derived from play for both children and parents, time for free play has been markedly reduced for some children'. Some of the factors they name as contributing to this decline include 'a hurried lifestyle, changes in family structure, and increased attention to academics and enrichment activities at the expense of recess or free child-centred play'.

This doesn't have to be the case in your home, however. Here are some things you might like to consider to foster an environment of play in your home:

- Think about where play happens in your home. Most children prefer to work or play close to their families, so if you spend lots of time in your kitchen or living room, that's probably where your children will want to hang out rather than in their bedrooms or in a designated playroom.
- With this in mind, it's great if children have a designated space to play in where their toys are kept and they can find what they are looking for. This might be a playroom, or their bedroom, or a corner of the sitting room or kitchen. It doesn't matter where it is, but it does help if it's a calm

space without too many distractions, with designated places for toys to be put away after use. Store toys so they can all be easily seen, keeping sets together in trays or shallow baskets. Low shelves or open storage units tend to work better than bins, trunks or large baskets as children are more able to find what they are looking for and then put them away again afterwards.

- If your children are a mix of ages, consider buying locking boxes to keep small parts such as beads, LEGO, or other choke risks out of the reach of little hands. Building on trays or in tubs can also help to safeguard creations from smaller siblings; when play is over, they can be moved onto higher shelves or surfaces.

- Arrange things so screens aren't the focus of your space. I definitely don't think that parents need to take a strict zero-screens approach — my own young daughter watches a little carefully chosen TV most days — but limiting the amount of TV to certain times of the day can help children find the space and, yes, boredom, that is needed to spark deep play. This might mean rearranging your space so that your TV isn't at the centre of the living space. Many families, including ours, live without television sets, instead using laptops, which can easily be put away, to watch shows and films on.

- If your space allows for it, keep one area for calm play — this might be the bedroom — and one for messy or noisy play — this might be the kitchen or living room. This means children who need some space can work on different projects and games without getting in each other's way.

- With younger children especially, leaving an invitation to play for them to find in the morning can be a great way to buy you time to have a quiet coffee first thing. Perhaps it's a dinosaur scaling a pot plant, a train track set up in your living space, or a teddy bear's picnic. Even older children can enjoy invitations to play, craft, make, build, and invent. I sometimes leave my daughter little drawings on the dining table for her to colour in while I make breakfast.

- If you have an outdoor space such as a garden, terrace, or balcony, find ways to make this safe and appealing, perhaps with access to water, sand, dirt for digging, pollinator friendly plants, and space for growing fruit and vegetables (a lot can be grown in small pots and tubs), and allow free access if possible.

Toy rotation

When it comes to encouraging deeper play with fewer toys, a simple but effective solution which works well for many of my clients is toy rotation.

It's easy to think that more toys = more play. But it's been shown in studies — and observed by many parents! — that having too many toys out at the same time can lead to a worse quality of play. This is because lots of toys can lead to children feeling overwhelmed by indecision; decision fatigue is a real thing — it's why so many adults feel stressed out by a long restaurant menu or endless arrays of similar-but-not-quite-the-same pairs of jeans. Not being able to find what they are looking for — or see what they have, for that matter — also creates mess, as children pull out toy after toy, dumping out piles onto the floor. If you've ever seen a child play for half an hour with a peg, or a simple doll, you will know that children don't need hundreds of toys for deep play. I truly believe that a few carefully chosen, open-ended items, and space to play are worth far more than a huge jumble of unsorted toys.

This is where toy rotation comes in. Carefully rotating toys and books — keeping some out and some put away — can lead to:

- A reduced number of choices your child has to make, reducing the stress they may feel.
- Deeper, richer, more imaginative play.
- Toys feeling fresher, novel, and more exciting.
- More independence for your child, as they can find, take out, and put back toys and books of their choosing.
- A calmer, more beautiful, less chaotic environment for the whole family.
- Less time spent tidying up — always a good thing — and less time spent searching for toys.

Toy rotation is always worth considering, but if you're in a period where you're spending more time at home I would venture to say it's a must. Not only will it encourage your children to play more deeply and keep your home feeling less chaotic, but there will be less need for new toys and books as you can simply bring old toys out into rotation, saving you money and meaning you use fewer resources. Everyone wins!

Four steps to better concentration and deeper play

1. Observe your child

Before you embark on your toy or book rotation, take some time to observe your child — and your space — carefully over a few days. Which spaces are working well, encouraging deep play? Which spaces always seem to end in chaos? How does your child engage with what is currently out? Do they have any favourite items which are often reached for? Are there any toys they consistently ignore even though these are accessible? Do they play for long stretches, or get easily bored and frustrated? Can they independently access what they need? Do they need to dump out other toys or books before reaching what they are looking for? Does everything have a space where it is put away every time?

2. Sort

Once you've observed your child, you can begin with the real work of toy rotation. I recommend starting with anything you want to get rid of (and by that I mean out of the home, or in long-term storage, rather than out of rotation). I would include anything broken, anything which your child has outgrown, any unnecessary duplicates, and anything which encourages violence or conflict. I also recommend looking at whether or not a toy requires your child to be active — make up a story and use their imagination — or passive — merely pressing a button or flicking a switch to make the toy light up or make a noise.

Next, think about which toys or books you want to keep out. For babies and young toddlers, you might keep out only a few things, whereas pre-school and school-age children may need more to keep them busy. What toys you have will vary hugely depending on your child and their age, as well as the space available to you, so I won't be prescriptive. I do recommend having a mix of open-ended toys — such as building blocks, balls, and playsilks — and toys for imaginative play — such as animals, cars, train tracks, and dolls. Infants may enjoy rattles, teethers, and items encouraging sensory exploration, and older children might like materials such as microscopes, globes, science kits, and access to writing materials to post letters to friends. If you have an older child, involve them in the process and ask them to think about what toys and materials they want to keep out.

For books, you can employ a similar approach. Are there any books you deeply dislike, or which promote messages which don't fit with your values? Do you still have board books out when your child is enjoying longer stories? We keep out a mix of seasonal books, fiction, non-fiction, and poetry. For both toys and books, be guided by your child's interests, and consider overlap — for example, a book or two on sea life and a basket of sea animals for a child who is a budding marine biologist!

It can be tempting to keep out everything your child shows an interest in, but remember — you're not putting things away forever, only until next rotation.

3. *Store*

Now you've decided what you want to keep out and what you want to put away, it's time to decide where everything should go.

Things you're keeping out:

My preference is for open shelving, with toys separated by type and stored in baskets, trays, or directly on the shelf, with only one type of toy per basket and bigger items (such as train sets or soft toys) in bigger baskets directly on the floor. If shelves aren't a possibility, then baskets on the floor or on a dresser can work well, and if you're finding it hard to source baskets, then things like wooden salad bowls, wicker fruit bowls, and even Tupperware can work well. For books, open-fronted bookcases are wonderful, as are baskets, picture ledges and spice racks. Your child should be able to see and reach everything by themselves — for a baby, this might mean having a very low shelf, a low basket, or even a few toys on a blanket or tray on the floor. For an older toddler or child, you could consider adding a stool to make things more accessible.

Things you're putting away:

If you have the space, a garage, cupboard, or wardrobe works well for any toys or books you are taking out of rotation, as it's more accessible than a loft but not on display. If you don't have that space, you could try putting things in a closed trunk or hamper basket, a big open basket covered with a cloth, on a high shelf, or under a bed or sofa. Try to keep sets of toys and seasonal books together so they are easy for you to find when it comes to the next rotation.

4. Observe again

Once you have made the changes, take time to observe again. This is perhaps the most important stage. With fewer toys out on display, you should be able to clearly see what your child is reaching for, and which toys or books are not sparking interest at that moment in time. Your child may well also tell you what they think, perhaps asking for a toy or book which has been put away. If they do ask for something which you've stored, it's fine to follow your child's wishes and get it back out — after all, the point is to make the space work for them!

Careful observation means that when it comes to the next rotation, it will be easier for you to see which items to leave out, and which could be stored away or passed on.

I have found this process invaluable, and it works just as well for toys as it does for books, art materials, educational materials, and even clothes. Once you've implemented toy rotation, you are likely to see changes in how your child engages with their toys and space pretty quickly. However, the clue is in the name — rotation! So it is a process which you will need to repeat over and over.

How often you rotate will be down to your child, their age, their interests, and their development. I have had periods where I have done several rotations in a short space of time, because my daughter Frida was going through a big developmental leap or suddenly had an interest in something. I have also had many long periods where nearly nothing has changed, because it was working well. Don't be afraid to experiment.

Sometimes children will ask for a toy which has been put away (I would say yes, as the whole point is to keep toys out that they want to play with), but in all of my time working with clients, I've never once heard of a child whose enjoyment and play hasn't been enriched through toy rotation. Once they can see what they have, and they have more space in which to play, children are usually delighted to 'rediscover' their toys.

It is really easy to fall into the habit of keeping everything out on display, especially when it comes to beautiful books and toys, or alternately shoving everything into big bins or baskets to keep them out of sight. If you haven't tried toy rotation, I urge you to give it a go and see. I hope you will be pleasantly surprised.

The power of simplicity

In our hectic, modern lives, it's no wonder that minimalism is a growing trend. We are overwhelmed by stuff, and it is taking from us our time, our space, our money, and even our joy. But you don't have to be a minimalist to enjoy the benefits of simplifying your home.

Simplifying is not about white walls and empty shelves. Our home is full of books, plants, art materials, piles of blankets, and jugs of flowers. You can be maximalist — colours! prints! piles of stuff you love! — and still live a simplified life. It certainly doesn't have to mean throwing everything away. Simplifying is often conceived of as physical simplicity and decluttering. But the hard work of simplifying is not usually the visible work which goes on. Thinking hard about our schedules, spaces, and expectations can often bring up unexpected feelings and dilemmas. Simplifying is an inner process as much as an outer one.

There is so much pressure to provide our children with all of the opportunities. From playdates to toddler ballet classes to the latest 'educational' toys, there are countless enrichments open to children today. But rather than enriching children's lives, too much of a good thing can lead to some seriously overwhelmed and exhausted kids. And it's not just our children. We are also over-scheduled, and more stressed and overwhelmed as a result, none of which is good for us or our parenting.

We know this, on some level. So why do we continue to pack out our schedules and fill the toy box? FOMO (Fear Of Missing Out), the anxiety that we or our children will somehow miss out on important opportunities, plays a big part. What if our kids grow up furious at us because they weren't given the chance to be a gymnast at the age of five? Will they be behind the other kids if we don't sign them up for Mandarin classes? Bluntly put, we say yes to things we know deep down won't really serve our families because of fear of saying no.

For us as parents, simplifying our home spaces allows us to feel calmer and more relaxed. Clutter isn't good for us. When our homes reflect our values, our tastes, and our needs, we feel better. And when we feel less stressed, we are able to parent more calmly. Less time cleaning, shopping, and tidying = more time playing, reading stories, and enjoying one another's company. In short, simplifying our homes creates more time for everything else. For our children, having simplified home spaces can help them to feel less stressed and overwhelmed. They can find their toys and know where to replace them, and they aren't confronted with hundreds of options when it comes to choosing something to play with or read. Calm, clear spaces allow them to deeply focus on their play without constant visual distraction.

The benefits of simplifying

I spoke with Bethan Henson, a writer, minimalist, and home-educating mother to two school-age children, about the positive changes decluttering can bring:

'I love simplifying because what we have in our home is an authentic reflection of what's truly important to our family. Decluttering can seem like such a daunting task, but the most joyful question to ask ourselves when faced with our belongings isn't "What do we need to get rid of?" but "What do we wish to keep?" What is precious, what is used, what matters most?'

Bethan, who runs the blog *Someday Slower*, continued:

'Before I started decluttering, I felt like I couldn't breathe. I couldn't function having mess everywhere, and it felt like motherhood was one long session of tidying. So we did capsule wardrobes, and got rid of the toys that weren't being played with. There's a real thing with decision fatigue in kids, and I was finding that when they had loads of toys, they'd throw everything on the floor and say they were bored. But when they had less, they started playing for hours. It was incredible. The children are so much happier, and I have so much more time to be present with them. We're sold the lie that kids need more, but the fewer the toys, the deeper the play. They are much more engaged now there is less, especially when it comes to home education.

'When I decluttered, I found another life underneath my stuff. I found a me I didn't realise was lost, but minimalism brought me back to the me I truly was.'

When you simplify your children's lives, you may find they feel more connected to you, feel less overwhelmed and stressed, display fewer 'disordered' behaviour and tendencies (the book *Simplicity Parenting* by Kim John Payne makes a powerful case for this), get on better with their siblings, and play more deeply and independently. Simplifying is also an important step towards fiercely protecting their childhood from the relentlessness of modern adult life, and it can help to reduce the conflict in your home around cleaning and tidying.

But the benefits of simplifying go further than the children. When you simplify your life, you may find you feel more connected to your family, calmer, and more patient, and have more time (to play with your children, to pursue your interests, to spend time with your partner). You might also find you have more money at your disposal, have more energy, and even feel healthier physically and mentally.

I have found time and again that, for young children, having less is truly more. But even the most minimalist of families will want to have some toys and materials in the home.

Toys which will stand the test of time

When choosing toys or materials for your child, here are some things to consider to ensure the toy will be loved, used, and provide you with good bang for your buck!

- How does this toy fit with your child's current interests and developmental needs?
- What is it made from? Natural materials — wood, silk, wool, cotton, metal — are often more pleasing to children's senses than plastic or synthetic materials. However, there are many plastic toys which are wonderful, so don't discount them altogether.
- How can the toy be used? Is it open-ended? Will it be used in imaginative play? Can your child project their own stories and feelings onto it?
- Does it fit with your values? Wooden swords, knights, or soldiers? Make-up sets? There's no right or wrong choice, but it's worth thinking about the messages your purchases send and if they are consistent with your family values.
- Can it be found pre-loved? Children don't mind, and it can be kinder to the planet — and your pocket!
- How was it made and will it last? Where possible, is the quality good enough that I can imagine passing it down to grandchildren, or is it going to break and be thrown away in a year?
- Is this item disrespectful to other people or cultures? What does buying a toy 'teepee' or headdress say about the

sacred items of that culture? How is diversity represented in play-sets?

Some of my favourite toys

The most important thing when choosing toys is your child's interests. It doesn't matter if everyone on social media has a toy rainbow, or a particular learning material: if your child isn't interested, it won't be a good purchase! That said, there are certain toys and materials which tend to go down well in most families. Here are some of my recommendations, tried and tested by my daughter, as well as many of my clients:

- Building materials: wooden blocks, magnetic tiles, Duplo/ LEGO.
- Figures: animals, people, small dolls, perhaps with vehicles, furniture, farm, or other accessories depending on your child's interests. These might be plastic, wooden, or fabric. Playmobil is a good place to start if you're feeling overwhelmed by choice, and I love Schleich for realistic animal figures which can take heavy play and still look good — these often turn up second-hand, and they last well.
- Modelling materials: playdough, modelling clay, air-dry clay, plasticine, and kinetic sand are all great, plus a selection of sticks, cookie cutters, sequins, googly eyes, stamps, rollers, and other loose parts (see below) to use. I love kinetic sand because, as long as it's contained in a tub or tray, it's relatively mess-free!

- Age-appropriate loose parts: a variety of blocks, pebbles, rocks, sand, shells, pine-cones, conkers/horse chestnuts, acorns, fabric scraps, pieces of string, shoelaces, lace, ribbon, beads (glass, plastic, ceramic), buttons, 'gemstones', marbles, twigs, pieces of wood or branches, cloths or silks, pegs, curtain rings, bottle lids, pipe cleaners, corks, ice lolly sticks, cinnamon sticks, nutmeg, nuts, seeds, clean fruit stones, kitchen implements, cutlery, scoops, balls ... the list is almost endless. Just ensure your child cannot choke on items you leave out, and always supervise children playing with small toys or loose parts. These can be used to tinker with, build, use as props in imaginary or small-world play, and so much more.

- Toys that develop gross motor skills: scooter, balance bike, pedal bike, balls, balance board. If you have an outdoor space then a trampoline, swing set, or slide can all be fun.

- Toys for imaginative play or roleplay: cloths, old sheets, scarves, or playsilks (use with pegs to make dens, to dress up with, or as landscapes for small-world play), dressing-up outfits (thrift stores, charity shops, and op shops are a great place to find these), doctor or vet sets.

- Water play items: plastic tubs, kitchen pans, spoons, cloths, and plastic or tin cups all work well for water play, and you can add herbs, dried flowers, leaves, grass, and other nature finds, as well as sieves and funnels for making 'potions' outside or in the tub.

- Puzzles: start with simple knobbed puzzles for young toddlers and work upwards.

- Games: there are so many to choose from, but from

pre-school age onwards your child may enjoy playing simple games such as Uno, Snakes and Ladders, and Bird Bingo. There is a huge range of games out there catering to all ages, stages, and interests.

- Simple musical instruments: rattles, drum, whistle (but be warned: though your child may enjoy this, you may not, so think twice!), xylophone, glockenspiel, simple percussion instruments.

Some children may also enjoy things such as:

- Doll, clothes, and crib
- Soft toys
- Toy kitchen
- Train set
- Toy till to make a shop
- Sewing kit

If you're looking for educational materials which will deepen your child's formal or academic learning, I'll be sharing some of my favourites for all ages in the next chapter. But for all children, play is one of the best ways they can learn.

Cultivating your home to encourage independent play

'How can I get my child to play independently?' is probably the question I am asked the most in my work! And I get it. Not only do we want those wonderful benefits that come from true self-directed play for our children, but we also would quite like them to play without us for a little while so that we can work, read, catch up on chores, or drink a hot coffee.

These are my tried and tested tips for encouraging children to play a little longer on their own:

Give your child lots of quality time with you if you want them to play alone.

It might sound counterintuitive, but I have found that children play much better once they have had some one-on-one time, and they feel safe and content in their attachment. This is probably the most important thing you can do if you'd like your child to be able to play alone. I have certainly noticed this with Frida: she is far more likely to play alone for a significant period of time if we have been reading together or playing together first. It's like her reserves have been built up, ready for her to spend some time without much interaction from me. I know how frustrating it can feel when you just need half an hour to get something done and you *really need* your child to play alone, but I promise they are far more likely to do so if you can give them your undivided attention for a while first. Having the kind of rhythm I described in Chapter Two — balancing in and out 'breaths' — can really help with this.

Provide time for unstructured play and exploration, and build it into your daily rhythm.

Building copious time for free play into your daily rhythm from when your child is still a baby will lay the foundations for a habit of play. Equally, it's important to have realistic expectations, and remember that all children are different. Some babies might not spend more than ten minutes at a time occupying themselves, whereas some will lie for a good 45 minutes trying to roll, or reach a toy. It's the same with children of all ages. I've met two-and-a-half-year-olds who can play for an hour by themselves, and six-year-olds who can't sit alone for more than ten minutes. Some children will naturally find it much easier to play alone, and some find it much harder and need more parental involvement. It's the same for feeling comfortable playing when parents are out of the room. All children will have different needs and will play in different ways! Consistency and patience will help with building the habit of independent play.

While they are playing, stay close but busy.
This helps children feel safe and connected — if you're nearby, they don't have to break their play to come and seek you out — without you distracting them. Reading, knitting, catching up on some nearby chores, journalling, mending holes in clothes, sorting laundry, sitting quietly with a coffee — all of these things work well for holding space for children's play, and of course if you need to work then by all means pull your computer out (but be prepared for this to perhaps be a little more distracting for your children at the beginning until the rhythm is established).

Provide toys and materials which spark their imaginations.

I'm a huge advocate of open-ended toys; toys with the potential to spark a child's imagination, and which entice the child to pick them up and play with them. A few simple toys are likely to see your child play far more deeply than toys which have done all the imagining for them. For babies, think mobiles, simple grasping toys made from natural materials, and mirrors to watch themselves. Young toddlers who are yet to play imaginatively may enjoy items such as treasure baskets, jars to open and close, stacking cups, and simple puzzles. I also love 'loose parts' for children to play, build, and tinker with (age-appropriate, of course). One of Frida's most used and beloved possessions as a toddler was a basket filled with pieces of wood, conkers/ horse chestnuts, cheap semi-precious stones I bought from the Natural History Museum, and pebbles. She used these all the time, and they become different things every day. Even now, she always has a 'treasure basket' out and available. These loose parts encourage so much creativity, even more so than many toys.

Respect their play.

If we want our children to learn to value their play, then we must show them that *we* value their play. If your child is happily playing, think carefully about whether you need to disturb them. Do they need to eat right now, or could you wait ten minutes? Could you change their nappy once they are finished? Can you hold off on bedtime just until they're done with the book they're reading? By interrupting our children mid-flow, we teach them that their play is not valuable. When you extend to your children the same courtesy you would show another adult who was immersed in a task, perhaps warning them that they will be needed soon and giving them a chance to wrap up what they are working on, you show your children that their play matters.

With this in mind, rethink what play 'should' look like.

Clue: it's not always sitting on the floor playing quietly with trains or dolls. Play might be loud, or active, or messy. It might look like climbing on furniture, or dancing, or painstakingly taking everything out of a bag and putting it back again five times in a row. As long as children are in that magical state of flow, it's play.

Limit screen-time.

I have found both personally and professionally that there is often a positive link between limiting screen-time and increasing independent play. I certainly don't think families need to ban screens altogether — they can be wonderful tools for learning and fun, and a lifeline for many busy, tired parents — but having a rhythm around when screens are used can help children play more deeply during the rest of the time.

These things won't guarantee your child will now play for hours on end by themselves (and they may well want to remain physically close to you in any case while they play). But I hope they will help you find ways of weaving more time for independent play into your daily rhythm — and that you get that hot coffee you deserve.

Toys, Play, and the Prepared Environment summary

- Simplifying your home environment and making space for beauty can increase play, reduce stress and conflict, and make life more pleasant for everyone.
- Consider your children's needs — how can your home meet these needs, whatever size space you're living in? Can you move furniture around, create an art space, or add a step-stool for more independence?
- Creating 'yes spaces' in your home allows everyone to feel more relaxed; you feel more at ease knowing your children are unlikely to do serious damage to anything, and they feel less frustrated.
- When it comes to toys, less is more. Open-ended toys and materials which encourage imagination and concentration will have more longevity than toys with one narrow purpose, or branded toys which will go out of favour along with that show.
- Toy rotation can help you keep your space clear and uncluttered while deepening your child's play — and reducing the need for more toys.
- If you want your child to play independently, give them more one-on-one time before you need them to play alone. Some children will find this harder than others, but by providing them with an engaging environment and staying close by, you're giving them the best chance of doing so.

Chapter Four

Awakening your child's natural curiosity

In order to learn effectively, children need a strong connection to their parent, caregiver, or teacher. They also need the security a predictable rhythm brings, and an environment set up for exploration and play. Without even thinking about formal learning, you've already covered the basics needed to successfully educate your child at home, whether it's your long-term plan or you're filling a gap caused by a house move, illness, or other unforeseen circumstance.

But, as we will see in this chapter, the most effective learning can look very different to how we might imagine it.

Natural born learners

Children are born learners. You're a parent — you've seen this in action. From day one, children are soaking up the world around them, making sense of the sounds they hear and sights they see, and figuring out how to move and use their bodies.

As Peter Gray writes in *Free to Learn*:

'Children come into the world burning to learn ... Within their first four years or so they absorb an unfathomable amount of information and skills without any instruction.

They learn to walk, run, jump, and climb. They learn to understand and speak the language of the culture into which they are born ... All of this is driven by their inborn instincts and drives, their innate playfulness and curiosity.'

Children learn all of the time. They learn in ways which we traditionally recognise — reading, listening to instruction, practising sums on worksheets — but also through play, tinkering, experimenting, having conversations, watching other people carry out tasks, and having hands-on experiences of the world around them. We tend to assume that, once they reach school age, children need formal instruction in classrooms, because that's overwhelmingly the norm. But if we look at families where children have never been to school, we observe deep, dynamic, enthusiastic learning and expertise.

Alan Thomas and Harriet Pattison write in *How Children Learn at Home*:

'When children start school, a dramatic change takes place in the ways that we want them to learn. The informal "as and when" learning of life is replaced by curricula, timetables, set lessons, teaching aims, testing and monitoring, because these are deemed necessary for continued satisfactory learning.

'There are however a growing number of children who never start school ... Many of these children carry on with, or return to, the informal learning which served them so well in infancy.'

Children are learning new things every day, whether they're at home or in school, through formal instruction and through their own discoveries. But just because our children are capable of learning by themselves, it doesn't mean that parents don't need to be involved. One of the best ways we can enrich our children's education is to build their knowledge of the world around them, giving them pegs on which to hang facts and experiences.

Knowledge is king

Knowledge allows us to make sense of the world around us. The more we know, the more we're able to learn and assimilate further knowledge and understanding. When we learn something new as adults — say we learn about a new politician, or historical event, or author — we will often start to see references to that thing or person everywhere, as if by chance. Of course these references were always there, it's just that we passed over them before as they were unfamiliar. But once we gain the basic information, we can deepen our understanding and begin to build a fuller picture of that subject. The more we know, the more we build connections between the different things we know, and the better we understand the world. It's the same for children.

Homeschooling — however long you do it for — provides a unique opportunity to build up your child's knowledge of the world, knowledge which will give them the context for all future learning. Free from the constraints of classroom curriculum, which especially in the younger years focuses heavily on reading, writing, and maths, children are free to dive deep into a broad and rich feast of ideas including myths, fables, art, science, history, geography, gardening, the natural world, and anything else which piques their interest.

And not only is this feast of knowledge valuable for its own sake, but it directly helps with reading comprehension; children have more chance of understanding what it is they are reading because they can place it in meaningful context.

As Natalie Wexler asks in her book *The Knowledge Gap*, 'What if it turns out that the best way to boost reading comprehension is not to focus on comprehension skills at all but to teach kids, as early as possible, the history and science we've been putting off until it's too late?'

Homeschooling can be easily structured to enrich children's education through building knowledge of the world. Two great ways to build this knowledge are:

1. Experience and hands-on learning where the child is able to witness things — such as a spider spinning a web, or ice melting — for themselves.
2. Reading widely and deeply about anything and everything, which helps both to deepen understanding or direct experiences (Why does ice melt?) and open up new knowledge the child cannot experience first-hand (Who were the ancient Greeks?).

Watching documentaries, planning hands-on research projects, and having conversations with knowledgeable adults — i.e. you! — are all ways of deepening this knowledge too. Together, these elements provide children with a strong, broad knowledge base about the world around them. And it's this base upon which they will stack all future learning.

Raising scientists

Children are born scientists. From the baby who drops toast from their highchair to see what will happen, to the child blowing bubbles in their juice, children are programmed to be curious about the world around them. And when we have our children home with us, we have an amazing opportunity to encourage that sense of natural wonder.

I spoke to Dan Green, the editor of *The Week Junior: Science and Nature*, a science magazine for school-age children:

'There is a "child as scientist" mode that kids go through from a really young age. My baby is just starting to drop things when you give them to her to see what happens to them, and I know soon she's going to start knocking things over in her highchair, which on some level is annoying as a parent but it's also really cool to watch her finding new ways to learn about the world around her. If you can encourage children to keep exploring, keep curious, and keep asking questions to find out how they world works, then they will do that and keep doing that, whether they define themselves as scientists when they get older or not.'

Dan, who has authored many science books for children and has three young children of his own, continued:

'That natural curiosity is there already in children, so you don't really need to do that much. You just need to be there to offer up different ways of doing things they haven't considered before. I recently dug a tin can into our garden with my five-year-old to make a mini beast trap, and then made a little grid in it so he could record his findings, and every day he's really enjoying drawing what falls into his trap. He loves finding out more about the creatures that fall in, too — far more than I would have expected. I've found that if you can give children different ways to explore and expand their curiosity, they will go further with it than you'd imagine.

'There are formal things you can add onto this natural exploration too if you want to take it further; if you're looking at a caterpillar or spider, then you can learn the names and functions of their different body parts, which is going to be genuinely interesting for children whose natural reaction will be "What is this wriggly thing and what is it doing?", or if you're making cardboard boats — which is basically an art and crafts activity, not a science one — you can explore if they float, and then test other things around you, which leads onto further discussion around why things sink or float. Just keep encouraging that "why".'

You don't need to do science experiments with your children to encourage their curiosity about the world around them, although they are fun too. Simply encouraging their questions, admitting you don't have all of the answers, and finding ways of learning and discovering together is enough. Children are so full of wonder and awe, and there's not always time to ask questions or follow their interests at school. Offering your child the space to ask 'why' time and time again is one of the most precious gifts you can give them.

The impact of stress

One thing we know is that children, like adults, cannot learn effectively if they are stressed. Long-term stress has a proven impact on the brain's ability to make and retain long-term memory — crucial if all of those books and lessons are actually going to stick — and we now know that the same thing happens with short-term stress, too, with researchers from the University of California finding that 'short-term stress lasting as little as a few hours can impair brain-cell communication in areas associated with learning and memory'.

Yet a 2018 survey from children's charity Barnado's found that school is the biggest source of stress for young people. This is borne out by my conversations with teachers around the country, many of whom describe children as young as six and seven suffering from anxiety, panic attacks, and feelings of low self-worth. This, they report, is getting worse over time, not better, and this anecdotal evidence is supported by research conducted in 2018 by the Australian Council for Educational Research (ACER) and Melbourne University which found that the mental health and wellbeing of school students is significantly worse than it was 15 years ago, with nearly half of Australian students reporting feeling 'very stressed'. This stress does not make for an optimal learning environment.

As John Holt writes in *Learning All the Time*, when he describes how children need to feel security before learning to read:

'Whether you are a "gifted" five year old or a terrified, illiterate twelve year old, trying to read something new is a dangerous adventure. You may make mistakes, or fail, and so feel disappointment or shame, or anger, or disgust ... The typical classroom, with other children ready to point out, correct, and even laugh at every mistake, and the teacher all too often (wittingly or unwittingly) helping and urging them to do this, is the worst possible place for a child to begin.'

Far from being second-best, your home is actually one of the best places for learning to happen; it is likely to be the place where your child feels most relaxed, safe, and comfortable. When stress melts away, information is effortlessly retained. However, even with this knowledge, it can be easy for parents to introduce unnecessary stress because we feel our children need to 'keep up'. No one is immune to the worry that somehow our children are falling behind some invisible, intangible golden standard. But this is something we need to be mindful of: if our children are stressed at school, at least they can come home and relax. If our children are stressed and they are homeschooled, there's nowhere for them to escape to at the end of the day. Imagine living with a teacher you didn't feel treated you fairly; no one wants that experience for their child! This is why in Chapter One I spoke about connection and relationships being the most important factor in successful home education: if our relationship suffers, then the home stops being that safe haven.

So how can we reduce education-related stress while homeschooling? Here are some guiding principles:

Don't push your child too hard.

No maths equation or handwriting sheet is worth damaging your relationship over. Remember that you and your child are on the same team: they are relying on you to support them when things get tough.

Weave moments for connection into your day.

As we saw in Chapter Two, creating a rhythm for your day means you can ensure plenty of moments for connection in your daily life, through meal times, reading aloud, and moments of focused time to learn and play together.

Allow for learning to be joyful, leaning into your child's natural desire and ability to learn about and explore the world around them.

If you're feeling the pressure, take a day to observe your child with a notebook and look for all of the ways they are naturally learning. For example, if they are building a train track, they are using engineering skills. If they are sharing out sweets equally between siblings, they are dividing. Reading a comic? They are still reading! Having a conversation about how butterflies come from caterpillars? Natural science. Making up rude poems? Literacy skills. You'll probably find that you have to abandon your notebook halfway through the morning, as you'll have so much to write down!

Take advantage of the lack of alarm.

One of the great things about homeschooling is being able toss out the alarm clock. Multiple studies have shown that the average school day is simply not designed to accommodate children's need for sleep or their optimal sleeping times. Tired children make for grumpy children — and grumpy parents — which in turn leads to more stress.

If you are going to do structured learning, keep lessons short.

School lessons may be an hour, but once you factor in setting up, packing away, disruptions, bathroom breaks, questions from other pupils, and waiting for help, the time spent actively doing formal learning is far shorter. Add to this that you don't need to teach a class of thirty, but can focus on one child at a time. Short lessons of ten or fifteen minutes help children retain focus, avoid exhaustion, and mean more time for moving, playing, and resting between working hard. Even older children who can focus for longer by themselves will not need you to be directly 'teaching' for very long; Charlotte Mason, a pioneering English educator writing at the turn of the twentieth century whose work influences many home educating families, wrote that a child of between nine and twelve years old should only be doing formal lessons between nine o'clock and noon (which, she assured parents, would give ample time to include music, artist study, French, Latin, German, and nature study, as well as the more traditional subjects of English, maths, geography, science, and history).

Know when to call it quits.

Some days (or weeks, perhaps even months) just need to be written off entirely in favour of books, movies, art, snacks, music, and lots of unstructured play. The beauty of this is that your child will still be learning! These pauses give you a chance to reset your relationship without any pressure on either of you to achieve formal learning goals. You are their parent above all else.

Homeschooling, whether it's long-term or just for a few weeks to fill a gap, can provide you and your child with a wonderful opportunity to deepen your relationship and reset from the stresses of school and modern life. Although it can be tempting to want to go all in, with lessons scheduled neatly throughout the day and goals and targets to meet, the best thing you can do to support your child's effective learning is to remove the pressure. After all, we want children to fall in love with learning. They won't do that if they are stressed.

Unplanned homeschooling

Home educating can be amazing — it's the route our family has chosen after all, so I'm obviously a big believer in it — but let's be honest: it's not a journey most homeschooling parents choose to embark on because it's the easy option. Even if your heart has been set on home educating since day one, there are always going to be tough days and bumps in the road. But at least if you've proactively chosen to homeschool your children, your life will likely be relatively well set up for it with your work arrangements, childcare, finances, and home space organised to make it a success.

If you are suddenly thrown into homeschooling, perhaps due to sickness, or a crisis which makes attending school impossible, then the chances are that you will not have all of these systems set up ahead of time. Yes, this makes it harder, but there are still ways of making the most of this time together so that your children don't just survive but truly thrive.

I want to stress once more that homeschooling does not mean that you need to replicate school at home — no matter what anyone else is doing. Your children are likely finding this period as challenging as you are, missing their teachers and school or childcare friends, and finding the abrupt change in rhythm difficult to navigate. This is not the time to try to build a classroom in your home; your children do not need a school timetable or structured lessons right now.

No one is expecting you to deliver an education equivalent to school — or those who usually home educate — because your life won't be set up for that. Instead, focus on encouraging the natural learning opportunities that abound in everyday life, and giving your children the space to follow their own interests, play, dive deep into projects, develop practical life skills, and read and listen to books. This is also a great time to complement what they've been learning at school, rather than recreating it. Read picture books on great mathematicians and scientists, watch documentaries about ancient civilisations, go and look for tadpoles, make up poems and research famous artists, play games, read myths and legends. Your child has been given a precious gift: the time to go deeper into these subjects and restart school with broader knowledge.

Navigating the space between school and home

In the course of writing this book, I've spoken to many parents with children ordinarily in school, who have been forced to home educate at short notice and who have been feeling completely overwhelmed by the sheer number of worksheets and resources that their children's schools have sent home with them.

If you find yourself in this position, I deeply sympathise. Essentially, you're being asked to replicate school learning at home, without any of the structures in place which allow teachers to do it successfully. And, as some parents are finding, if you try to 'teach' your children like a teacher would, they will likely push back, making it stressful for everyone. Schools have to teach a certain way because they are teaching the same material to thirty different children at the same time, all with different needs; you simply don't need to do this with your children, as you can offer short bursts of focused time which is tailored to their development.

Your child's school may well have been sending you worksheets because they feel a responsibility to keep delivering some kind of education for your child. The first thing to do is just talk to them and check in on expectations: if the homework is making you both stressed and damaging your relationship, explain that you're not going to force your child to do work which is making you both miserable just for the sake of it. Most schools will understand.

If the school is really insisting, make a compromise plan with your child — it can work well to each pick one task a day that they have to complete, and then the rest of the day can be given over to different activities your child enjoys. If forcing schoolwork is pushing your relationship with your child into a negative place or creating additional stress, my advice would be that it's simply not worth it. Having a strong relationship with you where they feel safe and happy will stand them in a better position when they return to their usual setting.

Your child may well want to do some of this formal work, however, enjoying the connection to school and the sense of normality it can bring. But this still doesn't mean you need to approach it in a traditional way. If they are struggling with a maths sheet, pick just one question to do every day as they build their confidence. On the other hand, if your child is a maths wiz, give them the hardest questions only and stretch their knowledge with some further discussion or by using online resources.

If you have teens at home who will need to prepare for big exams in the coming years, or be working on coursework or assignments, it's less practical to say that this work should be optional. Instead, make a plan with them about how they'd like to tackle their work, and ask them what they need from you to make it succeed. Try to agree timeframes for each big task, then avoid the urge to check how much they are doing between deadlines.

Putting the 'home' in home education

If you're homeschooling, your child will need somewhere to comfortably sit to draw, write, and carry out projects. But that doesn't have to be a desk. Their 'learning space' could be the kitchen, the sofa, the coffee table, the garden, the floor, or their bed, depending on what they're busy with. Learning happens everywhere. As we saw in Chapter Three, considering your home environment more generally is a great way to encourage natural learning. Are there books and art materials like paper and pens available? Is there a space — on a desk, table, or floor — where they can stretch out and create big work? Do they have access to a digital device where they can take an online class that interests them, or chat to friends? Are they encouraged to be independent in the kitchen? If you have teens, creating a cozy space for them to work — away from the noise of younger siblings, if possible — can help them get into the right headspace. Install a lamp or string up fairy lights, buy them some noise-cancelling headphones, and make sure there's a steady supply of drinks and snacks nearby.

The very things which make our homes homey — access to blankets, hot drinks, and art supplies, with room to stretch out — are the things which create a comfortable, appealing environment to learn and explore. Your home can rival any classroom precisely because it's a home, not in spite of it.

Homeschooling 'kit list'

Here are some of my home education 'must haves', though, even if your child ordinarily goes to school, these are all things they would use in their free time as well and that you probably already have. Interests will vary from child to child, of course, but these are the basics I would struggle without:

- A wide selection of books. I would include a mix of fiction, non-fiction, reference books, poetry, and biography, as well as field guides to local flora and fauna. If you can't access your local library or purchase books, you can initiate book swaps with friends. You could also add some foreign-language books.

- Good quality art materials, as described in Chapter Three.
- A mix of toys that encourage deep play, as described in Chapter Three.
- A globe, wall map, or atlas.
- Basic science kit: binoculars; magnifying glass; prism; selection of magnets; bug viewer; seeds, compost, and a small pot to observe the plant life cycle; a few inexpensive children's science kits (these are great for rainy days when you don't have the energy or patience to plan anything). If you have the space and budget, a microscope can be a great addition as well.
- Maths materials: games, e.g. Snakes and Ladders or Uno; measuring tape; ruler; stopwatch (most smartphones have one); loose parts like pebbles and sticks for counting; scales.
- Adventure kit: a backpack with a torch, water bottle, notebook, cheap camera, and specimen jar. Older children might like to include a penknife, too.
- A device for watching documentaries, movies, or educational shows.
- A way of playing music, like a bluetooth speaker.

Depending on what kind of activities your children enjoy, a printer can be really useful as well.

Learning and play ideas for all ages and stages

Gifting your children a rich childhood full of wonder, exploration, and natural learning sounds brilliant. But putting it into practice, especially if your own education was anything but enchanting, can be difficult without some concrete examples to get you thinking along the right lines.

These lists are not exhaustive — this book would be double the length otherwise! — but I hope that they will help you as you navigate home-based education, whether you are a homeschooler or not.

Activity ideas for all ages

These suggestions will be as relevant for tiny toddlers as they are for teenagers, and are perfect if you have children of different ages in the home. They'll look different for each age; you may want to expand on the picture books you read your young child with related non-fiction for older children (for example, if you're reading your baby *The Very Hungry Caterpillar*, you could read to your older children about butterfly life cycles), or make a space for your toddler to work alongside your eleven-year-old's art project. Here are some ideas:

Sit down and make a list of all of the things they'd love to do over the coming weeks and months.
Stick it on the fridge where you can see it.

Read, read, read.

If all you did for three months was read aloud to your kids from a range of great books — novels, picture books, poetry, biography, comic books — and let them play the rest of the time, they'd thrive. There is copious research out there on the benefits of reading aloud to children of all ages, and reading aloud grounds and connects you as a family, too, however old your children are. I spoke to Ronni Ozpolat, a speech and language therapist and mother of four home-educated children, who said, 'The benefits of reading are immense. Ask your child what they would like to learn about and then facilitate that learning. Start by looking for living books; those that are rich in ideas and make the subject come alive. Forget worksheets and, instead, focus on discussing thoughts and ideas that materialise through reading good books together.'

Listen to audiobooks and podcasts.

These can be a lifesaver if you need to work or get things done around the house, and you can find lots of classics, as well as modern books and children's podcasts, too.

Free play.

Finland doesn't start formal education until seven, and play has been shown time and time again in studies to have enormous intellectual, physical, and social benefits (Whitbread et al., 2017). If your children are happily playing or occupying themselves, this might be a good time to leave them to it — schoolwork can wait.

Play games.

Playing board and card games together can build family relationships as well as developing maths, reading, and cooperation skills. And many children build and cement friendships through online games such as Minecraft.

Throw a tea party.

Bring books, games, snacks, and drinks, and pile the table with flowers, candles, or seasonal decorations. This makes ordinary learning feel very special, and can become a beloved part of your weekly rhythm for your children to look forward to.

Bake.

Having children home is the perfect time to build a baking habit. Try bread, scones, cakes, flapjacks, or biscuits. Older children can follow recipes, while toddlers will enjoy pouring, kneading, and stirring. Baking can include maths, reading, science, history, even art. And of course, it's a useful life skill to have.

Get outside if you can.

If you can get to some open spaces, then go for nature walks or hikes. Time in green spaces is proven to have huge mental and physical health benefits for young and old alike — the book *Last Child in the Woods* by Richard Louv makes for fascinating reading on this subject — with studies showing that access to nature helps us get sick less frequently, and heal faster. The Institute of European Environmental Policy reviewed over 200 studies for a

2016 paper which found that 'there is robust scientific and practice-based evidence that nature can contribute to addressing health and social challenges'.

Garden.

If you're lucky enough to have an outside space, then having your children home means more hands for weeding, planting, and digging. Again, getting into gardening is good for health, and the bacteria in dirt has been shown to be beneficial to the microbiome, too. If all you have is a sunny windowsill, dwarf peas, certain flowers, herbs, and many more plants can be grown indoors.

Keep active.

Have a living-room dance party, or pop on a free online yoga or sports class; I've seen classes for online ballet, PE, and so much more. Young children especially have a lot of energy and need to move their bodies, so you may need to think creatively about how you can support them to get their need to move met (as we looked at in Chapter Three).

Art and crafts.

Cover a coffee table and surrounding floor and walls with newspaper and gather together paint, crayons, notebooks, pens, paper, glue, tape, scissors, and recycling which can be used for junk modelling. Older children might enjoy journalling as well as art projects.

Take care of the home.

Having your children home is a great time for kids of all ages to learn how to cook, do laundry, wash windows, strip beds, care for plants, mop, vacuum, dust, meal plan, and generally learn how to keep a household running. Go slow, be patient, and enjoy the (imperfect) help. Even young toddlers will love to spray windows, wipe tables, pair socks, and help prepare food.

Children of all ages will be able to be involved in these activities, to different degrees. If you have children of mixed ages, your older ones will be able to teach your younger ones how to do certain things; this is great for the development of both the older child and the younger one, and their sibling bond.

A note on nature

The very best thing for people of all ages is to get out into nature. Time in nature has been proven in countless studies to improve physical, mental, and emotional health, as well as increasing academic achievement and reducing the symptoms of ADHD.

As Richard Louv says in *Last Child in the Woods*, 'Time in nature is not leisure time; it's an essential investment in our children's health (and also, by the way, in our own).'

But in times of uncertainty or crisis, getting into nature — parks, beaches, countryside — may not be possible. I spoke with Forest and Beach School leader Rachel Stevens, who shared these encouraging words:

'I'm so passionate about getting families outdoors as

I truly believe that there is a place for everyone to learn and connect with the natural world. It is proven that spending time in nature benefits mental and physical wellbeing in people of all ages. Part of the magic is that everyone's experience of nature is unique and that can be incredibly empowering, whether you are an adult or a child.

'It's important to remember that "nature" isn't a far-off place, you don't have to visit a beach or a forest. It's absolutely everywhere — outside your window, sprouting through paving, nesting in roof eaves — which means we can all experience it on a daily basis.

'The key is starting small; being in nature is not all or nothing. If you are unable to regularly get outside, try:

- 'Growing plants on your windowsill — cress is small, fantastically quick to grow, and rather tasty, too.
- 'Make yourself a "sit spot" by a window and see what you can see outside. Try to identify species of trees, look for different birds, play games with the shapes in the clouds, or chart the phases of the moon for a month.
- 'Bring some natural materials inside — twigs, pine-cones, and leaves are all free — and you can use them for play, art projects, or decoration. Getting a potted plant or bunch of flowers works beautifully too.'

Activity ideas for toddlers and pre-schoolers

Being at home with children of all ages will bring different opportunities and challenges. But the age group I'm consistently asked about more than any other is young children:

toddlers and pre-schoolers.

Whereas babies are usually happy to be held, worn in a sling, spoken to, given space to explore simple toys, and involved in the daily life of the home, and older children and teens may have more ideas about what they want to be doing with their time, toddlers and pre-schoolers may require a little more thought to set up with appropriate, stimulating activities (especially if you want to keep them occupied so you can put the baby down for a nap or go through more challenging work with an older child, or just take a quick coffee break).

If there's one thing you need to remember about toddlers and pre-school children, it is this: they are naturally busy people. I've lost count of how many of my clients have wailed in frustration about their younger children that they just don't stop moving! And I get it; when you're tired, it's easy to wish your child would just sit and draw for an hour rather than crashing about pretending to be a 'big, terrible dinosaur'. But the busyness you can observe in young children is normal — and healthy.

As Montessori educator Simone Davies writes in her book *The Montessori Toddler*:

'Toddlers' needs primarily consist of using their hands in various ways (their grasp, crossing the midline, carrying objects, using two hands together), practising gross motor movement, self expression, and communication. Montessori activities for toddlers fall into five main areas of activities: 1. Hand–eye coordination, 2. Music and movement, 3. Practical life [activities of daily life], 4. Art and craft, and 5. Language.'

In a nutshell: if you have young children, give them

opportunities to move their bodies, involve them in the practical activities of daily life, give them time to play, read to them, play audiobooks, talk to them about everyday life, and provide some toys for deep play, such as blocks or figures, so they can develop self-expression.

Here are some more concrete ideas for things your young child may enjoy:

- Water play. (Put down a towel first and add plastic cups/ washing up liquid/plastic toys, or, if you're outside, then grass cuttings, flowers, and leaves can be mixed to make a 'fairy soup'.)
- Playdough. Pull out safe cutlery, twigs, flowers, shells, leaves, animal figures, stamps, and cookie cutters to make this into a fun activity which also strengthens hand muscles ready for writing one day. Making playdough 'aliens' can take the pressure off children with perfectionist tendencies to make something realistic, as can playdough cupcakes.
- Putting things into bags and purses. Toddlers love this, so gather any small bags, purses, and baskets and let them fill and empty them.
- Linked to this, many young children love packing bags or suitcases. Pull one out and ask your child to pack for an imaginary holiday (or maybe for an indoor camping trip, complete with den). You could tie this into learning about another country at the same time with some books.
- Puzzles. (Simple knobbed ones for young toddlers and more complex ones for older children.)
- Small-world play with animals or figures. Use household

items, cardboard boxes, or any outdoor space as a scene; a piece of cardboard painted green and blue can be a field with a river running through it, a carpet off-cut can be the basis of a doll house, a patch of weeds can be a jungle.

- Sorting activities using objects or pictures: sink or float (with a tub of water), magnetic or non-magnetic, living or non-living, fruit or vegetable are all fun places to start.
- Play hopscotch (outside with chalk, indoors with Washi tape).
- Building with blocks or magnetic tiles. You can add figures, animals, loose parts, and scraps of fabric to bring this to life.
- Matching games. For example, objects to pictures (toddlers) or simple words (pre-schoolers).
- Playing with kinetic sand and moulds, shells, or other natural loose parts.
- Making potions in the sink, bath, or garden with food colouring, bicarbonate of soda, vinegar, and water — add pipettes, plastic cups, spoons, and pans for maximum fun.
- Painting and decorating cardboard-box houses. You could also make a puppet theatre, with tea towels for curtains.
- Cleaning the house, including moving chairs and toys out of the way to clean underneath them (this provides children with opportunities for 'maximum effort' heavy work, which is an important gross motor skills challenge for small children).
- Threading beads/pasta shapes (note: beads should only be for children who have stopped mouthing objects, and only ever under strict supervision).

- Simple sewing activities, with a blunt embroidery needle and aida fabric for a toddler and a simple needle and thread for a pre-schooler (only ever under strict supervision).
- Sticker books/wipe-clean tracing books. These are especially good if they have an older sibling doing school-work nearby so they can copy them.
- Cutting and sticking from magazines and newspapers to make a collage.
- Making an obstacle course with sofa cushions and chairs.
- Making a simple blanket fort for playing and snuggling in.
- Using stencils and ink stamps.
- Have a music area with some simple instruments and offer to record them playing or singing on your phone, then send to family members.
- Roughhousing (wrestling, play fights, chasing each other, playing the 'sock game' where everyone tries to remove others' socks while keeping their own on); this has been shown in studies to help children develop resilience, emotional regulation, and connection with parents, and to reduce and release stress and tension. Agree on stop meaning stop, though, and never tickle or wrestle without your child's consent.
- If far from family, ask grandparents to read books out loud or tell stories over video call software, and set up virtual family dinners where you all cook the same thing and then eat 'together'.

Young children will more likely than not want to play or work wherever you are, so if you need to work from home or sit with a younger or older child, make sure there's a space set up nearby where they can busy themselves in the security of having you close by.

Activity ideas for school-age children

If you have school-age children then you might feel pressured to give them a rigorous, structured education akin to school so that they won't get 'left behind'. But, as we explored earlier in this chapter, children are naturally expert learners. Having your children at home with you is a wonderful opportunity to allow them to take the lead on their learning! But just because you're following their lead, it doesn't mean that you won't need to be involved. As a parent, your role is to invite your children into projects, suggest ideas, provide interesting materials, give support and guidance, find brilliant books, and gently stretch your child's skill and understanding through thoughtful questions, demonstrations, and simplifying complex processes.

I caught up again with Annie Ridout, who you met in Chapter Two, as she and her husband both juggled working from home with unplanned homeschooling for their six-year-old and three-year-old, alongside looking after the baby:

'In terms of the children's learning, we read a poem — Patti Smith, Brian Patten, Christina Rossetti, Keats — on waking, and write down our feelings. This is helping at the moment, but we will continue with it when "normal life" resumes as it's such a nice start to the day. Then we gather at the kitchen table — one adult (taking it in turns), two older kids (baby napping) at nine o'clock. Here, we do some reading, writing, and maths. Then lots of free play, garden time, a daily walk. Afternoons, there's some screen-based learning for the older two. Then maybe singing, guitar, piano, art and crafts. We are used to being flexible, prioritising particular work tasks alongside the children's needs, and each day working out who needs to do what. And right now, this flexibility is key.'

This is a great time to take your foot off the gas and give your child plenty of unstructured time for play. But there are lots of enjoyable activities your child can do that will also support them in developing skills and knowledge, like reading, writing, maths, and science, as well as deepening their understanding of the world around them. They might like to:

- Write books (just staple some paper together to make a simple book, which they can write, illustrate, research, and design).
- Create a living-history project: they can interview people online, take photographs, write a diary, collect artefacts, film a documentary, and more. They can also read histories of other times to compare.
- Write or draw letters to family.
- Video-call friends or family.
- Build LEGO projects (you could set them daily challenges).
- Try origami (lots of free tutorials online).
- Make cereal box dioramas and create objects out of air-dry clay or modelling wax to go inside.
- Learn to knit or crochet (if you can do this, then it might be a nice quiet activity to teach your children to keep their hands busy while they listen to audiobooks).

- Make stop-motion videos (there are many free-to-access guides and courses online).
- Act out plays (or write their own) with stage directions, costumes, lighting, and music.
- Make a fairy or gnome garden in a shallow dish with some grass or cress seeds, a little cardboard house, a 'pond' with a ramekin of water, and anything else they can find (again, lots of inspiration online).
- Watch nature documentaries and then illustrate or write about what they've learned.
- Read the book of a film/TV show, then watch the show and talk about differences in the two; write from the perspective of one of the characters; make a set out of a cardboard box to recreate their own scene.
- Simple sewing projects like making clothes for dolls.
- Science experiments. There are lots of ideas online for simple science experiments you can do using kitchen ingredients, or you can buy inexpensive science kits.
- Learn a language together as a family. Learning a language has heaps of cognitive benefits, no matter your age. Buy a beginners' guide, and learn three new words a day! The Duolingo app is free and easy to use.
- Take an online class or watch an educational video. Some ideas include Outschool, Mystery Science, BBC Bitesize, ArtVenture, Khan Academy, Scholastic, Kid Lit, National Geographic Kids, and TedEd.
- Draw around the outline of their body on paper, then have them label/illustrate their body, perhaps using some books as a reference point.

- Explore philosophical questions together. There are some great books out there, such as *Big Ideas for Curious Minds* from the School of Life, which you can read together and use to spark conversations about what it means to live a good, wise life. But you don't need a dedicated book — fairy tales, story books, and plenty of films and TV shows will prompt questions about how people should act and treat each other.

Many of the suggestions for younger children will still be appealing to school-age children — they may be able to do these independently or take the ideas further, or even teach younger siblings! And, as with younger children, the best thing you can do for your school-age child is to encourage their passions, read to them a lot (yourself or via audiobook) from a variety of great books, and provide them with time and space to explore their interests.

Children of this age will love being given time to follow their interests, whether it's dinosaurs (where my daughter is currently at), volcanoes (like one of her friends), or church bells (like another of her friends)! Being able to go deep into what they love will naturally bring opportunities for all kinds of learning, whether it's finding out about fossils and how different rocks are formed, the history of Pompeii, or how sound is created by vibrations.

If you're homeschooling for the long haul, then you may want to start introducing some elements of structured learning from age six or so: short, practical lessons on foreign languages, maths, science, and more. But if you're homeschooling to fill a temporary gap, then the best thing you can do is expand your child's knowledge, and give them time to play, potter, explore, and be bored. This is your opportunity to give them an extra slice of childhood.

A few words on teenagers

If you find yourself with teenagers at home, you might be wondering how all of this applies to you.

Supporting teens stuck at home

I spoke to Maria Evans, a secondary-school teacher turned coach for teenagers, and mother of three, about how parents could support their teens at home:

'My first piece of advice would be to establish a rhythm, just as you would with younger children. Teenagers also like to know what their day will look like and what to expect. Rhythm and structure — however that looks for your family — helps young people feel safe.

'Next, can you find a way to help your teen become part of a bigger community? Perhaps a choir or amateur dramatics? Something that will make them feel part of a family outside their domestic one, where their contributions are needed and appreciated. This has such a positive effect on their self-esteem, and it's fun!

'Third, can you find opportunities for them to succeed? This can be something quite small such as chores around the house, to something more challenging such as preparing a meal for the family on a regular basis. This is excellent for boosting self-esteem, as well as teaching teens important life skills.

'Lastly, allow them tech and a social media presence. Research has shown that young people who have no access to smartphones are more unhappy that those who spend a small amount of time online each day. Set the boundaries together, follow your teens on their social media platforms, and teach them about how to be safe. Connection with friends and being up to date with their pop culture is very important.'

If you find yourself home educating your teenager, the best thing to do is sit down with them and make a collaborative plan for any learning goals. Consider together: what do they need to get done (revision for exams, deadlines set by external teachers), what do they want to get done (what would they like to spend more time exploring), and what do they need from you to make this happen (space to work, materials, support with certain areas, access to an online tutor for a certain subject).

There are many free online courses offering fantastic tuition around a wide range of subjects. The Open University, Coursera, and Khan Academy are just some to consider. Being at home is also a good time for them to explore their passions. Maybe they want to film a documentary, or start a podcast from their bedroom? Master the guitar? Write a novel? Design and sew clothes? Build a computer from scratch? Learn to bake sourdough? Take a car apart and put it back together?

Working together to create a framework will ensure you're

both on the same page, and keep those important communication avenues open.

Home education, not school at home

I hope these ideas have gone some way to showing that home education — whether you are in it for the long haul, or just as a temporary measure — can open up learning possibilities for your child far beyond the realms of what they are offered at school. Your child has a unique opportunity to develop their knowledge, interests, and skills, and the benefits of this period of time will most likely stay with them for the rest of their lives. You really don't need to be a teacher to give your child a top-quality education. You just need to know them, love them, and trust in their ability to learn.

Socialising when you can't go out

Whether your child usually goes to childcare or school, or they are ordinarily home educated, providing opportunities to socialise with others is key. Usually, homeschooling families provide broad socialising opportunities through playdates, groups, learning co-ops, classes, visiting friends and family members, and going about daily life; meeting new people in playgrounds, supermarkets, and museums. Homeschooling is not just about staying home!

But when circumstance dictates staying close to home, providing opportunities for children who want to socialise with their peers can be tricky, but it's vitally important. Younger children may be happy spending long periods of time just socialising with parents and siblings, but older children will often crave the social interaction of friendships.

Give them the time and space to chat to friends and family on regular video calls (building these into your daily or weekly rhythms), and perhaps through collaborative age-appropriate games such as Minecraft. You may need to relax screen-time limits a little to ensure that this can happen. I wouldn't worry too much about this, though — it's not forever, and chatting to friends is far less passive than other forms of screen-time. Ensure you've spoke to your child about what is okay to share online and what isn't, and go through basic safety rules such as never chatting to strangers, telling people your address, or saying things online you wouldn't say to their face. If you have teenagers, make sure you're giving them privacy to chat wherever possible, again perhaps scheduling in this time so they know when they can expect some time alone to speak freely to friends and romantic partners.

For non-screen-based activities, you could suggest writing letters to friends and dropping these round if they live locally, or emailing if you want to reduce postage. They could include pictures, photos, nature finds, quizzes, and plans for future fun.

I know from experience that it can heartbreaking and worrying watching our children miss their friends and family. But finding creative ways to support your child's friendships will make a big difference to how they feel now — and later.

Homeschooling through crisis: a note for home educators

Even if you ordinarily home educate, if emergencies or unpredictable situations occur, it's likely that your family won't be completely shielded from the impact on your daily life. A house move, an adverse weather event, a health pandemic — all of these things can throw your usual rhythms and plans out of the window. Your children may not attend school, but mass closures will still affect the groups, classes, co-ops, playdates, and other outings and activities which make up the backbone of many homeschooled children's weeks. They will be missing out on social activities as much as their friends who attend bricks-and-mortar settings, and when navigating these challenges it's important to remember that it's okay to slow down, shift gears, and cut yourself — and your children — some slack.

Comparing your homeschooling in difficult times to how things were in more normal times is only going to make you feel frustrated. Instead, lean into the reasons you chose to home educate in the first place. The freedom to go at your own pace, the ability to let your children pursue their own interests, the time to read great books cover to cover, the chance to teach life skills like gardening and baking alongside physics and Latin; these are all principles that can guide you through these uncertain times.

I want to remind you that it's okay if your children do nothing but listen to audiobooks and play for a while as you find your new normal. As a homeschooler, you already know it's the moments which don't look like any real learning is going on where the magic often happens. If things are feeling overwhelming, put the curriculum away, pull out a pile of your best read-aloud books, bake a cake, and call time on formal school for a while.

Julie Bogart, American author of *The Brave Learner*, home-schooling veteran and mother of five adult children, recently wrote of home education during the COVID-19 pandemic:

'Education — learning — is not an emergency. It's not even urgent. So if you feel yourself ramp up, or are worried that your child is behind, or wonder if your child is learning enough, ask yourself if that isn't the anxiety from this odd moment spilling into your home school. Because my hunch? It likely is. And then, deliberately slow down. The best learning happens when we are patient, adapt the lessons to a child's capability, and provide kind support. When everyone is preoccupied by a threat to their existence, it's no wonder we all feel a little distracted, disoriented, and behind. But those feelings aren't about learning.

'If you're finding it hard to get it all done, go back to baby steps. One ten minute session today — draw a subject from a hat. Then tomorrow, try ten minutes in the morning and ten in the afternoon. Do that for a few days. Rotate subjects, until you've covered them all. Now is a time to "go slow to go fast".'

Supporting sibling dynamics

If you have multiple children, then helping them to build sibling relationships which will allow them to spend all day at home together is a crucial building-block of successful home education, whether you've been home educating for ten years or ten days. And if your children have previously been in school then this work will be even more important, as they learn once again how to live alongside one another day in, day out.

I asked Nicole Kavanaugh, a Montessori blogger and host of the *Shelf Help* podcast, about her experience helping her four children (currently aged between six months and nine years) to develop strong relationships. She said:

'It is through play that children explore their surroundings, their social dynamics, and learn. If you want your children to become good friends, they have to play together. This play will fuel their bond and strengthen their friendship. But, if you want your children to play together, they have to have something to play with. If you only have toys with specific aims meant for specific ages, they aren't going to find those opportunities to be together. If something is too frustrating for the younger child, or not engaging to an older one, they won't find each other in play. A basket of blocks, some toy animals, art supplies, or a dolls' house can ensure that they all have their role. While they may not be playing the same game at the same time, or playing with the same level of detail, they can both adapt their play to their needs while being together.'

She added:

'You need to let their relationship happen. As parents, we need to step back and allow them to make connection, find their common interests, and develop a bond without our interference. You need to respect that they have their own relationship. Just like you have a relationship with each of them, your friends, and your spouse, they have a relationship, with its own dynamics outside of you. They are going to have disagreements, they are going to have times where they drift apart, and they are going to have other relationships that compete with their own. And they have to navigate these challenges. You need to lean into the lack of control over their relationships.'

When children are learning together, here are some more things which will allow positive relationships the space to develop:

Trust in their goodness.

Even when things are really, really hard. Remember that they are doing their best right now, and how small they are.

Find time to do things together, like art projects, reading aloud, and nature walks, but also get creative with having one-on-one time with each child.

Do more challenging work with older children while the baby sleeps, and snuggle with the littles ones when the bigger kids are playing a game or working on independent projects. Have dedicated one-on-one time with each child for things like reading and maths, and then have them both listen to audiobooks, watch documentaries, and work on science experiments. Many older children relish the chance to play 'teacher' with their younger siblings, showing them phonics or simple maths, or teaching them basic vocabulary in another language.

Stay away from comparison.

The comparisons that parents make between siblings can harm not just the relationship with their child, but they can undermine sibling relationships too. It's natural to compare your children, but try not to let this spill out into your parenting. If you hear yourself about to make a comparison, take a deep breath and count to ten.

Allow all feelings.

It might be hard to hear that your firstborn hates their new brother and wants to send him away, but rather than saying, 'You don't really mean that, you love him really,' give them a safe space to express themselves. Although having siblings can be wonderful, it can also be hard on children who feel they have rivals for their parents' affection. Accept that all feelings are valid.

Notice moments of warmth and connection between siblings.

It can be easy to focus on the challenging moments, but take time to soak up the moments of kindness, however short!

Listen to everyone fairly.

Sometimes it can be easy to jump to your own conclusions before you've heard the full story. When there is an argument or someone has hurt someone else, take a deep breath, pause for a moment, and then listen to what each child has to say (if they are verbal), keeping neutral and sportscasting or repeating back what you hear.

Give siblings space to work things out.

Show them that you trust them to forge the relationship that works for them. Rather than immediately jumping in to arbitrate or put an argument to an end, wait and see if your children can solve the problem themselves, perhaps while you sportscast. Sometimes the resolution reached may not be what you would have chosen, but try to respect the decision your children have made together.

But don't be afraid to step in.

Especially if one sibling is bullying the other or someone is at risk of getting hurt. If someone does get hurt, try apologising, 'Sorry I didn't step in sooner, I didn't realise quite how upset and angry you were feeling.' This removes some of the guilt and shame from the child who was aggressive in this instance.

What to do when everyone needs you at the same time

You've finally sat down to work through some maths with your eldest when your toddler starts shouting for a snack, waking the baby, who starts crying. One child wants you to read while the other really, really wants you to play trains with them. Your twins are both experiencing some big feelings after an argument and both need your support. Does any of this sound familiar? Although it would be great if each child could always have your undivided attention exactly when they needed it, that's often not going to be possible (this is even true for one-child families!).

So what can you do when both children need you?

- Prioritise safety. If there is a risk of someone getting hurt, you may need to physically separate them for a short time and go back and forth between them until calm is restored. A child who is physically hurt may need attention first.
- Don't be afraid to go back and forth. Sometimes all you can do is give each child your focused attention in small doses.
- Sportscast — a lot. 'I can see that you're both really upset right now and you both want me to hold you and not the other. That must feel really hard. It is hard for me too, as there is just one of me and two of you and I really want to help you both.'
- Prioritise needs, and try to anticipate needs when you can. A child needing the toilet takes precedence over a child who really wants to read a book or play. Get your pre-schooler set up with drawing before you help your older child with their writing, or get your toddler a snack before feeding the baby. You can't always plan these things, but the more you can, the smoother things will feel.
- Find ways to reconnect all together. Sharing a good book, putting on some music for a dance party, reading aloud, going into the garden for a run-around, putting on a movie — anything which will bring calm back to your family when everyone is having a hard time.

Building your child's motivation

How do we encourage motivation? This is a question I'm sure all parents ask ourselves at some point, from encouraging our children to tie their laces or brush their teeth to working through tricky maths problems or handing in college assignments on time.

The answer is actually relatively simple: our children are motivated to do things for much the same reasons as we are motivated to do things. They are motivated by things which interest them, which have a practical purpose, or which have meaning. It's why so many children struggle with schoolwork which doesn't interest them, doesn't seem to serve a practical purpose, and doesn't feel important to them.

If you've ever seen a baby trying repeatedly to stand up, a toddler determinedly filling a basket with every single block they can find on the floor, or a child reading until way past lights-out because they can't put the book down, you'll know that children come with huge amounts of motivation already built in.

When it comes to offering learning opportunities, motivation is less about what we say, and more about how we present things. Are we finding new, fresh ways to present ideas? Are we tying new concepts into things our children are already interested in? Are we showing them how what they learn can be applied to practical, everyday life?

Leah Boden, a homeschooling mother of four children, shared with me that she had been showing her youngest children how to create a pie chart to represent how many cups of tea each member of the family drank throughout the course of the day. Just a small shift like this made the concept so much more relatable than if she'd asked them to represent data irrelevant to their family life. There's a reason so many homeschooling families talk about learning science and maths through baking: it's a practical skill with an identifiable outcome, and most children like to eat cake and biscuits!

There are two things, however, which, although commonly used by parents and teachers, don't motivate children in the long term: praise and rewards.

The problem with praise

Instinctively, many parents feel that praising their children and rewarding 'good' behaviour is the right way to communicate love and pleasure, build a child's confidence, and encourage the adoption of positive habits and behaviours. However, as we shall see, not all praise is equal.

We can see praise and rewards are two sides of the same coin. Rewards tend to be physical — toys, stickers, chocolates, physical affection — whereas praise is usually verbal, although it can be written, too. They act in much the same way, so we will look at them together.

Praising our children's outcomes, comparing them to others, or giving person-centred praise like 'you are smart', 'that was so clever', and 'well done' can lead to what is called a fixed mindset. This is a belief that qualities such as intelligence and the ability to work hard are fixed and innate, and our actions will not impact them. Even for children who are thriving academically, this kind of praise can lead to a fear of failure and an avoidance of risk due to an internal pressure to succeed and keep feeling smart. Effort can make those with a fixed mindset feel stupid, as they feel as though they should just 'get' things because they are naturally smart. They can end up doing things because they want praise and recognition; the praise is the end goal, not the work or activity itself.

Conversely, encouraging children to work hard and put in effort, or commenting positively on the process rather than the finished product ('I noticed how hard you tried') can support a growth mindset. This is a belief that intelligence is fluid, and can be grown and developed by putting in effort, working hard, and not being afraid of making mistakes. Challenges are embraced because they lead to learning. Research suggests that simply teaching children the idea that the brain is a muscle that can be grown through working hard — in other words, equipping them with a growth mindset — can lead to better grades (Blackwell et al., 2007).

Growth mindset

In a famous study by Claudia Mueller and Carol Dweck, children were given an easy task to complete. The group was then split in two; the first half were told that they succeeded because they were smart, and the second group were told they succeeded because they put effort in and worked hard. They were then asked to choose another task to complete, one of which was easy and one more challenging. Those in the second group were more likely to choose the task which was challenging and which would stretch them, but the first group were more likely to choose the 'safe' easy task. The groups were then asked to self-report their scores; the second group exaggerated their results by 10 per cent, whereas the first group exaggerated by 40 per cent. The majority of children praised for their intelligence asked for information about how their peers did on the same task, but not even a quarter of those who had been praised for effort asked for this type of feedback — most of them asked for feedback about how they could do better. We see here that labelling children as 'smart' or 'clever' may actually cause them to underperform, rather than boosting their confidence and leading to more success.

The erosion of intrinsic motivation

As well as leading to a fixed mindset, praise and rewards can erode children's internal, or intrinsic, motivation: rewarding someone for doing a task can actually make them less likely to complete that task successfully. An interesting study (Grusec, 1991) found that four-year-olds who were praised for 'prosocial' behaviour such as helping were less likely to behave in this manner than children who were not praised. Other research has shown that children who are praised for being 'nice' are less likely to think of themselves as nice people, and are less likely to help others when there is no reward (including verbal praise) attached, and that external praise and rewards reduce intrinsic motivation for children of all ages, from preschoolers to college students (Kohn, 1999; Deci et al., 1999).

Praising children can lead to children — and subsequently

adults — being 'hooked on praise' (or, more specifically, the dopamine hit that comes from being praised), and focusing on how people will react to their actions rather than on the tasks themselves and the internal satisfaction doing something well can bring. They become less able to take pride in their own accomplishments and lose persistence, quitting when rewards disappear. Praise removes the child's focus on how they feel about their behaviour, actions, or work, and focuses them instead on the person doing the praising; by praising or rewarding, even with the best of intentions, we are evaluating our children's actions and centring our own opinions. (I love what Carol Black says on this in her essay 'Children, Learning, and the "Evaluative Gaze" of School'.)

I have certainly witnessed the negative effects of praise myself. If I reflect back on my days at school, I was often praised and rewarded for doing tasks which came relatively easily to me, and told over and over again that I was 'clever'. When I went to Cambridge University as an undergraduate, I was suddenly shocked to realise that, next to my classmates, I was decidedly average. My confidence took a huge hit, and there was a difficult period of adjustment as I was faced for the first time with work that genuinely challenged me. Scared of failure, I put off doing work, procrastinated, handed essays in late. It took me a good couple of terms to slowly build my confidence back up. I can see clearly how well-meaning praise throughout my childhood created a pressure not to fail by external standards, and an avoidance of risk in order to keep the external praise coming.

How can I encourage my child without rewards?

But how, I hear you ask, can I get my child to do anything without praise or rewards? What about when they have to do things which don't naturally motivate them? Here are some things you can try which will help your child get things done while protecting your relationship — no punishments or shame here — and without damaging their motivation in the long term:

Model the desired behaviour.

This is the most effective thing you can do in the short, medium, and long terms! If you want your children to tidy up, be tidy. If you want them to speak calmly, do so yourself. If you want them to be kind, be kind to them and others. Have them see you brush your teeth, wash your hair, read, cook, or learn a new skill.

Be playful.

Play allows us to move away from control, towards collaboration and joy, and it has the happy result of being really effective in encouraging children to get things done too. Make up games, set challenges ('Can you put on your socks before I count to ten?'), speak in silly voices, get a favourite teddy to brush teeth together. Whatever works for them!

Bring things like maths, handwriting, reading and science to life in ways which will interest them.

Maybe your child doesn't want to write a report, but would enjoy writing and illustrating a comic? Could you recite times tables by throwing a ball to each other, or fishing for sums attached to magnets?

Build tasks into your rhythm.

Consistency is key. Tidying before moving on the next activity, washing hands before every meal, encouraging them to carry their plate to the sink after every meal. With repetition, these tasks can become woven into your daily rhythm and become accepted and embraced habits.

Use reasoning.

Even when children are very young, you can explain things to them. The older they get, the more they will understand and the more sophisticated you can make your explanations! If you want to encourage tooth brushing, tell them in an age-appropriate way about microbes in their mouth that cause cavities. If you want to encourage manners, explain that people prefer being spoken to gently and politely.

Tell them stories.

If you have a young child, talk about how you helped clean up every night as a child, or tell stories about a little animal or another child who didn't want to brush their teeth and how they overcame the fear of doing so and learned to enjoy it. With older children, seek out inspiring stories about people who did hard things and overcame challenges.

Reframe challenges.

If your child is struggling with something, help them see that it's okay to struggle because they're still learning. From around age three, you can start talking to them about their brain being 'plastic', and explain that the more they practice doing something, the easier it will be for them to learn.

Check your expectations.

Are your expectations developmentally appropriate? Is your child genuinely capable of doing what you're asking, or are you feeling external pressure to get them to do a certain task?

Sharing in your child's joy

A question I am often asked by my clients is, 'If I shouldn't use praise and rewards, how can I share in my child's joy and happiness?' Not praising or rewarding your child can sound pretty joyless. But just because you're not giving out constant praise, it doesn't mean you can't show your child how much you love and appreciate them.

There is a difference between:

1. Praising your child because you wish to reinforce or change their behaviour.
2. Factually letting your child know when something they are doing is correct when there is no in-built control of error, especially if they ask you to tell them. (For example, 'I think

this letter is a "F", is that right?' 'Yes that's right, it's an "F",' or 'Is my shoe on the right foot?' 'Yes, you got it right.')

3. Genuinely sharing in your child's joy and delight.

So how can you share your children's joy without praising them?

Pay attention to what they are doing, and show an interest in their play and work.

Showing your child that you are interested in them and what they are doing is the best way to encourage them, and demonstrates that you value their work and efforts. Making eye contact when they talk to you, getting down on the floor to play, observing them while they work, talking to them about what they are doing: these are all great ways of showing that you care.

Give evaluation-free statements instead of praise, and/or ask questions.

For example: 'Look, Mummy, I drew a dinosaur!' 'Oh yes, I can see that. You drew a green dinosaur. What is this bit of red here? What is the dinosaur's name? It makes me feel very cheerful to look at it, are you feeling cheerful?' Again, this shows you are genuinely interested in what they are doing.

Say thank you.

If your child does something helpful, say thank you, just like you would if another adult helped you out in some way. Remember, children are just smaller humans who deserve to be treated with the same courtesy you would an adult. You can get specific and say, 'Thank you for chopping that carrot for me. You chopped it really finely, which was exactly what I needed.' This is so different to saying, 'Good girl for helping!' As long as you are genuine in your thanks, then you can't really go wrong. Saying, 'Thank you for not dropping any more food on the floor' after you've asked them to stop is perfectly fine if you're feeling genuinely thankful.

Tell them you love them.

Not just when they do something which pleases you, but all the time. You cannot do this too much! Saying things like 'I love playing with you', 'I look forward to reading books with you', and 'I really enjoy spending time with you' often and with genuine meaning communicates how much you value your child exactly as they are, without praising them. It is especially important to remind them of your affection — through language, touch, and tone of voice — when you are enforcing a boundary or their behaviour is at its most challenging. This is when they most need to feel your love.

Do nothing.

Just allow them the space for their own satisfaction, without saying or doing anything. They don't need praise to feel the satisfaction of a new skill learnt, or a job well done.

Awakening Your Child's Natural Curiosity summary

- Children are born learners. You're a parent — you've seen this in action. From day one, children are soaking up the world around them, making sense of the sounds they hear and sights they see, and figuring out how to move and use their bodies.

- If you want to encourage your child's natural curiosity, welcome their questions, admit you don't have all the answers, and find ways of learning and discovering together.

- Your home is actually one of the best places for learning to happen; it is likely to be the place where your child feels most relaxed, safe, and comfortable. When stress melts away, information is effortlessly retained.

- Read, read, and read some more. If all you did for three months was read aloud to your kids from a range of great books, they'd thrive. Audiobooks are your friend too.

- Home education can open up learning possibilities for your child far beyond the realms of what they are offered at school. Your child has a unique opportunity to develop their knowledge, interest, and skills, and the benefits of this period of time will most likely stay with them for the rest of their lives.

- Positive sibling relationships which will allow your children to spend all day at home together are a crucial building-block of successful home education. Don't compare your children, but give them space to work things out, and find things they can enjoy making or watching together.

- Praising children's outcomes can lead to a fixed mindset, but encouraging them to work hard and put in effort, or commenting positively on the process rather than the finished product ('I noticed how hard you tried'), can lead to a growth mindset.

Chapter Five

Self-care for ordinary and extraordinary times

Taking care of ourselves is one of the most fundamental aspects of calm parenting, and yet perhaps one of the least discussed issues in books and articles on the topic. It's a vital foundation for all parents and caregivers: when our needs are met and we feel joyful, we can bring this joy to our daily lives with our children. Similarly, when we're feeling burnt-out and exhausted, we simply cannot show up the way we want to show up, as parents and humans.

We need to relearn how to cherish and nurture ourselves in the same way we cherish and nurture our children. We need to learn how to parent ourselves.

Looking after our needs is crucial if we are to be understanding and empathic with our children, connected to our partners, and happy and fulfilled as individuals. I think sometimes it is assumed that if you are to be a good parent then a certain level of martyrdom is required — that as a parent you must sacrifice your life for that of your child, always putting your child first while pushing aside your own desires, interests, and needs, and that anything less is selfish and irresponsible.

But here's the thing: it's impossible to be a calm, fun parent if you don't prioritise yourself from time to time.

It is much harder to be patient and stay calm with your children when you are exhausted.

It is much harder to stimulate your child's intellect when you're not looking after your own.

It is much harder to do the inner work that every parent needs to do, to unpick how you were parented and the impact this may have had on you, when you are burnt-out.

It is much harder to model to your children what a healthy, happy adult with diverse interests looks like when you don't make time for these things yourself.

It is much harder to cherish your time with your children when you feel resentful because your needs are not being met.

Your needs deserve to be taken seriously

When we become parents for the first time — whether we give birth, adopt, or become a step-parent — we get used to putting our needs to one side in order to care for our children and adjust to loving someone more than ourselves. But as we adjust to parenthood and our children grow in their independence and resilience, it can be easy to forget to reprioritise our own needs, and they can gradually get pushed to one side to gather dust.

But your needs deserve to be taken seriously, just as your children's needs do. You deserve time to yourself to pursue your interests and dreams. You are worthy of pleasure, time with those you love, and intellectual stimulation. Your body is just as deserving of being respected, nourished, and well rested.

It's harder when your children are very young, especially if they are breastfed and relying on you for all of their nourishment (and much of their comfort), or waking often at night and in need of support. Sometimes there is a 'needs collision' and you have to put your children first; this is normal. But this doesn't mean that all of your needs have to be put aside, all of the time. Parenting is demanding. As we explored in Chapter One, it requires tough inner work, and time to play and connect and respond to your children's needs. But it doesn't — and shouldn't — leave you with nothing left for yourself.

Modelling self-care to our children

Self-care is important for its own sake. But it's also important in the context of what you are modelling for your children. Take a moment to think about the messages you'd like them to soak up about their own worth and the importance of taking their needs seriously. Are you living this yourself? What message does it send your children when you serve them a home-cooked lunch, but you survive on coffee and their leftovers? Modelling self-care matters for them as well as you. It's why I feel no guilt when telling my daughter I can't play with her now because I want to read my book or take a bath. I want my daughter to learn that rest is important.

Fit your own oxygen mask first

It sounds counterintuitive perhaps, but the best thing parents can do during stressful, frightening, or uncertain times is focus on themselves rather than their children. There's a reason we're told to put on our own oxygen masks first, after all. Children respond to how we, as parents, react to uncertainty, and look to us for feelings of calm, security, and confidence in navigating radically changed patterns of daily life.

But I've seen firsthand over and over again in my work with parents around the world that, despite knowing this, self-care is one of the first things that parents let slip when they are busy, tired, stressed, or worn out. I have had many clients — often brilliant, intelligent women with interesting careers and passions — who, when I ask them what they do for themselves, simply can't think of anything. Or, like Katherine, a thirty-something Londoner parenting a three-year-old, they can think of a whole list of things they'd love to do, but by the time bedtime is over, the dishes are done, and work emails have been answered, they are so exhausted that they have no energy left for themselves.

It seems easier to read more books, schedule more coaching sessions, or buy more stuff than it is to simply slow down and address our own needs. I say simply, but of course you know there is nothing simple about getting your needs met when you are juggling the needs of everyone else around you.

Making space to meet your own needs will help you to effectively process your own feelings; building a framework of self-care practices will mean you are more able to continue your work — both paid work and parenting work — perhaps without external support from family members, childcare, or schools.

What exactly is self-care?

What images come to mind when you think of self-care? A bubble bath? A manicure? A glass of wine? Watching TV? A marketing slogan?!

None of these things is the wrong answer, necessarily; I love taking the time out of my day to have a hot bath and read a book, and all the better if it occasionally comes with a glass of wine (though don't look at the state of my fingernails because manicures do not make my list). But I think that this somewhat stereotypical understanding of self-care can simplify the idea beyond the point of usefulness, turning it into a caricature which many parents simply cannot relate to.

Fundamentally, self-care is about finding ways to get your emotional, physical, mental, and intellectual needs met. So a bubble bath may help you meet your need for rest or for time alone but it's not a magic cure in and of itself, only insofar as it helps you meet your needs.

Self-care will look different to everyone; it should be based on you. Your current unmet needs, your interests, your desires, your hopes and dreams, your personality — all of these will define what good self-care might look like for you.

I believe that self-care has to include taking care of your mental health, including seeking professional help if you have experiences you need to heal from; building and maintaining robust boundaries; doing the challenging but vital 'inner work' we all need to do to understand ourselves, our drivers, and our actions; checking in with our feelings and understanding how these present in our bodies; and showing up to ourselves with kindness and a sense of compassionate curiosity. Doing this inner work and taking care of our mental health can feel difficult at the best of times, and near impossible when things are tough. But it's precisely in these challenging moments that we need to take care of our headspace more than ever.

Self-care isn't always about adding more things, though. Sometimes the best self-care we can give ourselves is to remove things: relationships which don't serve us, commitments which are burning us out, physical stuff which is making us feel overwhelmed and causing our homes to feel cluttered, thoughts which are taking up our precious mental space.

When thinking about self-care, it can be helpful to begin by spending some time reflecting on what your needs are, as you began to explore in Chapter Three. Understanding and identifying your emotional needs is as important as taking care of your physical needs. Both types of needs are intimately linked: when your emotional needs go unmet, these can have a very real physical impact on you — as anyone who has had stress headaches or physical symptoms of anxiety or stress can attest — and vice versa.

Here are some questions you might want to explore:

- What do you need to feel happy at this point in your life?
- What do you need to feel healthy at this point in your life?
- What brings you into a state of 'flow'?
- When you feel anxious or stressed, what is usually missing?
- Which of your needs do you feel are currently being well met?

- Which of your needs do you feel are currently not being well met, and need some focus?

If you are struggling with this last question, think about whether there are any external signs that give you some clues about where your unmet needs lie — perhaps things you have been ignoring. What is your body telling you? Have friends or family expressed any concern for you? Are there unhelpful habits or behaviours you can observe in yourself which help to show what you are missing right now?

Know that you deserve care and pleasure

Before I go any further, I have to say something important to you:

> *You deserve pleasure and enjoyment even when you haven't 'earned' it. You deserve pleasure and rest even when the to-do list is still full.*

You are allowed to sit on the sofa with your book even when the kitchen is a mess. You can watch a movie despite not having bought your niece's birthday gift. You are allowed to go for a run even though you haven't finished cleaning. You can go to bed when the sitting room is still covered in toys.

When I truly allowed myself to believe this, it fundamentally changed how I treated myself. It allowed me to treat my own needs and self-care as just as important as, or even more important than, all the other things I needed to do.

When we defer pleasure until we've finished everything on

our list, then more often than not we go to bed exhausted and without having had the time for doing the things we actually wanted to do, the things which would leave us feeling relaxed, nurtured, and whole. I'm not denying that chores need to be done. But I am saying that it's important to put yourself — and your pleasure — first from time to time. You likely won't be given time, so it's up to you to create some.

Some ideas for self-care

You might also already have a clear vision of what you need. However, some clients I have worked with have fallen out of the habit of self-care to the extent that they have found it difficult to imagine what this could look like for them, beyond a massage or a glass of wine. So if you need some inspiration for self-care, here are some ideas, most of which cost nothing or very little. I want to stress that this isn't an exhaustive list; I really recommend doing the work described on the previous pages to dig into what you truly need.

Nurture your mind

- Read! (Not just parenting books! Read thrillers, literary fiction, poetry, non-fiction, a graphic novel, a newspaper, a cookbook …)
- Listen to audiobooks, podcasts, or the radio.
- Watch films, TV shows, and documentaries that stimulate you.
- Learn a new language (there are lots of free courses online).

- Take a free online course in a subject you've always wanted to try.
- Teach yourself a new practical skill, or enrol in a community class.
- Speak to your friends on the phone or see them in real life.
- Listen to beautiful music, look at art, book theatre or concert tickets.

Take care of your mental health

- Journal.
- Start a gratitude practice, listing 20 things a day you feel truly grateful for.
- Meditate and/or practice mindfulness.
- Treat yourself with compassion.
- Avoid bad news on the TV, radio, or online.
- Be in nature.
- Allow yourself space to feel grief and sadness if that's how you feel.
- Speak to your doctor about how you've been feeling.
- Go to therapy or counselling, or accept medication (this is self-care!).
- Go online less and take breaks from social media.
- Make things with your hands (bake, knit, craft, draw, garden, cook, sculpt, paint, crochet, build things, restore furniture, write, arrange flowers) and find that beautiful moment of flow.

Respect your body*

- Sleep.
- Dance.
- Run.
- Have sex.
- Call the doctor/dentist/osteopath about those worries you've been putting off.
- Swim (in open water if you can!).
- Do a yoga workout (there are lots of free apps and YouTube videos available).
- Try yoga nidra (a form of yoga which encourages deep rest).
- Eat delicious food which makes you feel good.
- Drink enough water.
- Get a massage (a friend or partner might be happy to do this!).
- Go for a walk.
- Take an uninterrupted bath or shower.
- Stretch in the mornings and evenings.

* I appreciate that not everybody will be able to do everything on this list, but I hope it gives you some ideas.

Create a restful home environment

- Pick or buy fresh flowers or grasses.
- Have plants in your home.
- Light candles, burn oils, open the windows.

- Declutter and make your home feel lovely, one small corner at a time.

Protect your boundaries

- Be fiercely protective of your time.
- Practise saying no more often to people or commitments that drain you (this is really hard but gets easier!).
- Put your phone on silent or just turn it off.
- Save your time and energy for things and people that make you feel good — your time is your most valuable resource, after all — and spend time with people who make you happy (drinks — virtual or in person — with friends, a date with your partner, reading on the sofa with your children, lunch with another family you like).

It's one thing to identify your needs and to know the sorts of things that would help you to fulfil these needs. But it's quite another thing to look at your life — full of chores, childcare, work, meals that need cooking and gifts that need sending — and know that you can actually get these needs met, so I'll share some tips for carving out time for yourself later in this chapter.

Sometimes self-care can feel like just another chore to add to the list, something we feel we 'should' be doing but never quite get round to, that we end up feeling guilty about instead. Sound familiar? In these situations, developing self-compassion can be one of the most powerful acts of self-care we can undertake.

Self-compassion

In Chapter One, I wrote about the need for adopting an approach of Unconditional Positive Regard (UPR) when we consider our children and their behaviour. I'd like to encourage you to develop this approach when thinking about your own actions, paying attention to the inner voice you use to speak to yourself. I like to think of this as 'compassionate curiosity'.

The way we speak to ourselves can be critical and unkind; we often speak to ourselves in ways we'd never dream of speaking to our children or lovers. We berate ourselves over small mistakes, agonise over perceived failings, compare ourselves unfavourably to others: 'I have no willpower', 'I'm a bad parent', 'I always do …', 'I never manage to …', 'Why am I like this', 'If only I could be more …'

Psychologist, lecturer, and leader of the Insight Meditation Community of Washington, Tara Brach, gets right to the heart of this in her book *Radical Acceptance*:

'For so many of us, feelings of deficiency are right around the corner. It doesn't take much — just hearing of someone else's accomplishments, being criticised, getting into an argument, making a mistake at work — to make us feel that we are not okay.'

She continues:

'The belief that we are deficient and unworthy makes it difficult to trust that we are truly loved … We yearn for an unquestioned experience of belonging, to feel at home with ourselves and others, at ease and fully accepted. But the trance of unworthiness keeps the sweetness of belonging out of reach.'

Our inner critics can have loud, powerful voices, amplified further by the guilt which so often accompanies parenthood. Often, these critical voices have been with us for years, even since childhood ('You're too loud!' 'Why are you such a show-off?' 'No need to be so shy'). But although it can be difficult to change the way you speak to yourself and view your actions, it is possible to reframe your response so that you view yourself with compassionate curiosity. Here are some things you could start to bring awareness to:

- Pay attention to how you speak to yourself. What is your inner voice like? Is it encouraging and gentle, or critical and harsh?
- Notice when you speak to yourself unkindly (without judging yourself for it). How would you speak to your child who was going through the same thing? Can you offer yourself the same empathy and warmth?
- Practise cultivating a genuinely compassionate curiosity for your actions. Rather than criticising yourself or asking 'why', simply note with interest what has happened, without trying to 'fix' or change yourself. For example, if you lose your patience with your child and snap at them, rather than piling guilt on yourself, offer yourself compassionate curiosity: 'That was not how I usually respond, or want to respond. How am I feeling right now? How is my body feeling? What needs of mine might not being met right now?'

- Remember to look at your behaviour through the lens of Unconditional Positive Regard. If you didn't act in the way you'd hoped you would act, perhaps you did so because, in that moment, that was the best you could do.
- Offer yourself a kind gesture when you feel that inner critic creeping in. Place a hand on your heart and take a deep breath, perhaps while thinking to yourself, 'I am doing my best.'
- Practise sitting with your emotions, even the uncomfortable ones. Scan your body, noticing if any parts feel uncomfortable or tense, and where you feel those challenging feelings. Labelling your thoughts and emotions allows you to realise that you are not your thoughts, nor are you defined by them.

Developing compassionate self-regard is a vital act of self-care. I think it's one of the most important things we can do. Sure, it's less tangible than going for a solo coffee, or having a kale smoothie, but honestly? Even if you go for regular runs, eat healthy food, sleep enough, and get time to yourself to socialise and nurture your interests (and if you are doing all of that, you're already doing better than me!), if you are speaking to yourself cruelly then you are still depriving yourself of the empathy and kindness that you truly deserve.

Something which can really help us in developing compassionate self-regard is mindfulness.

Bringing mindfulness to our lives as parents

The thing I love about mindfulness is that I can practise it anywhere, whether I'm alone or in the middle of homeschooling my daughter. If I'm feeling frustrated or overwhelmed, or I'm close to losing my temper, I can pause, take some deep breaths, and remember that I have a choice to react or respond. It isn't always easy, but I'm so grateful for the space and grace mindfulness has given me during my most challenging parenting moments.

As Susan Pollak says in her book *Self-Compassion for Parents*:

'Mindfulness doesn't have to be something you do alone in silence in a meditation hall on a remote mountaintop, but something that can become part of your crazy, busy life as a frantic parent trying to juggle way too much. Which is, in fact, when you need it the most.'

I spoke to mindfulness teacher Jodi Garrod about how parents can bring mindfulness and self-compassion into their lives:

'We now live in a world of "continuous partial attention" [a phrase coined by Linda Stone], always busy, always "connected" through technology, always scanning for our next and best opportunity. This "always on" lifestyle can leave us feeling overwhelmed, overstimulated, and ultimately unfulfilled. However, studies have demonstrated that we are actually happiest when our attention is fully engaged in the thing or activity we are currently doing.

'Our "continuous partial attention" is also damaging to our children, who thrive from us being fully present to them and their needs. Mindfulness provides us with this opportunity to be more fully present. On one level, it is a practice in training our attention or awareness. However, as our practice develops, we can think of it more generally as a way of first taking care of our own experience, and then attuning that care towards others, including our children. By giving our full attention to each and every moment we touch, we are actually imbuing each moment with our care.'

Jodi, who is also the mother of a two-year-old boy, continued:

'Mindfulness is the art of noticing, of truly listening. Paying attention in this way, we enter into a fuller relationship — a deeper intimacy — with our lives. Our thoughts, our feelings, and the sensations alive in this body. There is both a simplicity, and a depth, which arises from that. An openness, willingness, curiosity to be with what is here. Life becomes more rich, more textured, more free … and ultimately more joyful.

'The great power of mindfulness is to reteach us what it truly means to listen and to feel and to notice. We can be so busy being busy that often all we feel is overwhelm and deficiency. Mindfulness awakens us to how full and rich this life already is. We listen not only with our ears, but with our hands and our feet and our skin and our hearts. We remember that our entire body is rhythmically attuned to the whole of life. We remember that we belong.'

Simple mindfulness exercises

Jodi shared with me these two exercises, which are perfect if you want to bring more mindfulness to your daily life, but feel uncertain or overwhelmed about where to start:

1. STOP.
   Stop
   Take a breath
   Observe
   Proceed

This very basic mindfulness practice highlights how mindfulness gives us a choice to respond (wisely, with intention), rather than simply react to situations, emotions, or feelings.

This mindful pause essentially allows us to stop, take a breath, and step back from the turmoil of the situation and choose how we then move forward, with greater awareness.

We cannot always control the circumstances of our lives, but we can choose how we respond to them. Each one of us will encounter sorrow, suffering, grief, loss, and pain, but it's how we respond to that suffering which defines and shapes our lives. This mindful pause essentially allows you to stop, take a breath, and step back from the turmoil of the situation, and choose how you then move forward, with greater awareness.

2. Follow the sensations of the breath in the body.

Just noticing and following the sensation of the breath can be very profound for most people. The majority of people spend most of their time in their heads.

Observing the breath pulls you back into your body. Your breath is anchored in the present moment; when you follow the breath, you are developing 'moment by moment' awareness.

During a breath meditation you might:

- Notice the quality, texture, or temperature of the breath as you inhale and exhale.
- Notice the sensation of the body expanding on the inhale.
- Notice how it feels to release the breath on the exhale.
- Notice the wave-like motion of the breath: the way the inhale rises into the exhale, and then becomes the inhale again. You could say in your mind: 'Breathing in … breathing out' if it helps you to follow your breaths.
- You might also place a hand on the area of the body where you most easily feel the breath (such as your abdomen or chest) and observe the rhythm and flow of the breath there.

If you've never practised mindfulness before, these are great exercises to start with. Although it can feel a little daunting, as Thich Nhat Hanh says in his wonderful book *Fear*: 'Every one of us has the capacity to be mindful, focused, understanding and compassionate. That quality is inherent in everyone.'

I take great comfort in these words when I am feeling anything but mindful, remembering that the aim is not perfection, but practising a tool which can help me get through the tough days and thrive during the better ones.

Getting your needs met while parenting

As we've seen with mindfulness, self-care doesn't necessarily mean time away from your children (though you probably need that too, depending on how old they are and if you feel comfortable leaving them yet — if you don't, then listen to your instinct).

You can still be around your children and take moments to put your own needs first. You can leave chores during nap time, and rest. You can read while your children are playing. You can do a yoga routine while your child is around. You can take five minutes to drink hot tea.

As well as finding ways to put your own needs first while taking care of your children, you can absolutely find ways to meet your own needs while meeting your children's needs, too. Enter the glorious concept of Sites of Mutual Fulfilment, which we explored in Chapter Two. Simply making a list of these — and then making it a priority to do more of them — can be life-changing. They are the ultimate win when it comes to parenting, and the more you can fit into your life together, the more joy there will be all round.

Finding community

As Aristotle famously said, 'Man is by nature a social animal.' We not designed to spend long periods of time alone or in our nuclear family units. Much has been written about our need for a 'village', especially when it comes to parenting and raising children. This means that those periods of time when you're forced to spend more time at home without friends and family around — perhaps after having a new baby, or during a period of illness, extreme weather, or an unforeseen crisis which means you have to stay indoors — can feel even more lonely and difficult to navigate; it's precisely during the times that it's hardest for us to find community that we need it the most.

I spoke to Adele Jarrett-Kerr, a writer, home-educating mother of three, and host of the podcast *Revillaging*, about how we can find community when circumstances force us to be physically distant:

'Families continue to need "the village". The capitalist image of the self-contained individual upsets it, parents' own competitive schooling trains them out of it, and the many pressures of modern life have left little time for it. None of this changes the fact that to live in community is to express our humanity. Becoming parents is often disruptive and isolating under normal circumstances, bringing us uniquely in touch with our need for wider, deeper connections.

'When circumstance requires us to physically separate from people outside our households, the call to create community is even stronger. We need each other's support so we don't buckle under the unprecedented strain of isolation. Our children need to know that there's still a world out there. We're being asked to protect each other by doing something that runs counter to our human instinct. Yet there's potential to emerge from this, newly aware of what it means to belong to each other.'

I also spoke to Jenny Phillips, a mother to two young

children who lives in Scotland, about how she retained her community after her family relocated from the south of England:

'I've been physically distant from all my friends and family for nearly two years now, following a relocation, and these past few weeks [during COVID-19 restrictions] are the least distant I've ever felt in that time because everyone is in the same boat now and making heaps of effort, and for me that's been so strange — and nice!

'The things I try to do to keep those relationships alive are sending post, remembering key dates such as birthdays and anniversaries, having WhatsApp groups to exchange photos and offer support — this works especially well across time zones — video calls, cook-and-bake-alongs with grand-parents, watch-alongs where we watch a play or film series at the same time as friends, then video-chat to talk about it after (we did this with a play from the National Theatre for a friend's birthday recently), and Zoom or Google Hangouts meetings for special occasions — a group of friends had a virtual book launch for our friend this week because her real-life one couldn't happen, and this would also work for things like baby showers. One of my friends sent me a six-month flower subscription when we moved, and it was so touching and amazing. She even scheduled it to arrive on a Tuesday, which she knew was the hardest day in my week.'

I asked my online community for any other suggestions for staying connected to others during tough circumstances, and here are some of their ideas:

- Host an online book club.
- Co-counselling (sharing feelings and challenges in a small virtual group).
- Online workouts or dance classes.
- Create street or neighbourhood WhatsApp groups.
- Play games online together.
- Do meditation together.
- Invite others to virtually collaborate on projects such as gardening, redecorating or reorganising your space, and so on (I have friends I will call up to ask gardening questions, and another to whom I'll send photos of our home to get her advice on where things should go).
- Online 'pub quizzes', where people take it in turns to come up with questions each week.

These things won't replace a long hug with your best friend or a family dinner party. But they can help you through the most challenging moments: apart, together.

Creating space apart from your children

Although self-care doesn't necessarily have to mean time away from your children, at some point you will need or want time when you are 'off duty' — time that is just for you. This can be hard! Especially when your children are young (perhaps still nursing), if you're a single parent or your partner works long hours, when you don't have 'a village' who can support you, if you or your partner (or your children) have health conditions, when you don't have the disposable income needed for high-quality childcare or there are no high-quality childcare options available near you, or any combination of the above. And, as we have seen in recent years, sometimes due to a global crisis or natural disaster, having time away from children can become impossible.

With that in mind, here are a few tips and ideas to help you find little pockets of time to yourself, and build them into your daily and weekly rhythms:

Try to do chores when your children are awake.

This gives you naps and post-bedtime free for yourself (and if your child won't sleep without you lying next to them, I've been there, and I promise it doesn't last forever).

Arrange reciprocal playdates with friends, even if it's just for an hour or so.

This gives you some time child-free with the peace of mind that it's someone you know looking after your child.

Talk to your partner — if you have one — and schedule in regular time each week that you can have for yourself.

And do the same for them, as they also need time for self-care! Each of you having a few hours on a weekend morning to yourselves as well as a weeknight for you each week can give you both a decent chunk of time alone.

Take annual leave.

And keep your child in school or childcare! Just don't then

spend that time off doing chores. I know some couples who try to book regular days off together so that they can go on dates.

Take the sick days you are entitled to.
It's okay to rest when you need it.

Ask family for help.
This can be easier said than done, especially if your family lives far away or has a different approach to parenting than you (and of course this assumes that you have a positive relationship with your family, or that you're not physically isolated).

Do a 'time audit'.
This sounds very dull but it can be really revealing, especially if you feel you have no time to do the things you really want to do. Think about:

- How much time do you spend on your phone, or on social media?
- How much time do you spend watching TV?
- How much time do you spend doing chores in the evenings? What could be done earlier in the day, streamlined, or done less frequently?
- Who does bedtimes and the night-time routine in your home? Who gets up on weekends? Could you and your partner do alternate days so that the other gets a break in the evenings or mornings? (I appreciate that this is

an area single parents do not have flexibility around.)

- How do you spend your weekends? Do you need to spend every moment together? Could you go for a 15-minute run while your partner is reading stories or playing? How about taking your book and having a long bath while everyone else watches a movie?

Thinking critically about how you actually spend your time can be really useful for helping you identify time you might not have thought you had.

Get up before the children.

(If you have very early risers, are bed-sharing or room-sharing, or are being woken up at night, then this may be unrealistic for the time being.) Could you get up half an hour earlier than your children so that you can start off the day just taking care of your own needs before you become 'Mummy' or 'Daddy'?

Pay for help, if this is possible.

A babysitter, help with cleaning, getting shopping delivered if possible — all these things can gift you some time.

Communicating your needs around self-care can feel challenging, even more so when you're asking for help to create more child-free space in your week, or when you want to do something that costs money. It's easy to feel like time and money used for self-care is 'indulgent', especially when these resources can feel scarce during the earlier years of parenting. But remember that you are worth it. Consciously choosing to invest time and resources into your pleasure, fulfilment, and happiness can only have a positive impact on those around you. If you are burnt out, no one wins.

When communicating your needs to your partner, friends, or family members:

Ask clearly for what you need.

So often, we don't ask clearly and outright for what we need. 'I would really like to take an art class but it's on Tuesday evenings for a month — do you think you could clear space in your schedule to be with the children so that I can go?'

Reciprocate.

Help your partner, friend, or family member to get their needs met too. 'I'd really love a regular lie-in. How do you feel about getting up with the kids on Saturdays, and I could do the same for you on Sundays?'

Remember you are on the same team.

If you and your partner are in the throes of parenting, it can be exhausting and feel as though you are the parent who never gets a break (whether you stay home, go out to work, or a combination of the two). Evenings and weekends can feel like a 'needs collision' where you both desperately need a break. Remembering that you're on the same side can help you to work together to help each other get your needs met — the Nonviolent Communication principles discussed in Chapter One will help.

When your needs clash with your children's needs

What happens when your needs clash with your children's needs? This is something I'm sure you will be familiar with. You feel touched out; they want to feed. You are exhausted; they need comfort in the night. You are desperate for time alone; they want you to play.

Firstly, it's important to reiterate once more that your needs are just as valid as your child's needs. You matter too. That said, often your child's needs will have to come first, especially if they are very small and cannot wait long when they are hungry or in need of comfort, or unwell, or going through a challenging period where they need more support than usual. During these intense seasons of parenting, our needs do sometimes go unanswered as we tend to the smallest members of our family.

But even during those long or weary days, a little planning and thinking about your needs can go a long way. Having a jug of water and a basket of snacks next to your favourite feeding spot, a five-minute meditation with headphones in while the baby naps and the pre-schooler watches a show, asking your partner to support you in getting to bed early or sleeping in a little in the mornings, saying yes to people's offers of help — all of these things can make a difference. In moments where you have more energy, spend a few moments brainstorming a few things that can help you feel nurtured (a cup of hot coffee on the front doorstep first thing in the morning to get some fresh air before anyone wakes up, a dance party to music you love with a cranky baby in a sling). Again, thinking about Sites of Mutual Fulfilment can really help here, too.

Spending some time thinking about where your needs clash with your child's needs can be helpful in figuring out some creative solutions to ensure that your needs don't get completely sidelined as your care for your children. Just because your children's needs are more urgent at times, it doesn't mean that your needs vanish.

When your children get older, they can begin to wait a bit longer for some of their needs to be met, and you can begin to place your needs a little more prominently in the picture.

This might look like asking your partner to do some bed-times so you can have time to yourself in the evenings, even when you are the 'preferred' bedtime parent. It might mean eating a sandwich before you give your children lunch so that you're not going hungry, if you feel you cannot eat at the same time. It might look like nursing a toddler less frequently because you're feeling touched out and need some physical space. It might mean creating a quiet-time rhythm when your child drops their nap so that you both get some time to rest in the day, and maintaining a limit around how available you are during that period of time. It might mean getting a babysitter or booking your child into childcare so that you have a little bit of time to yourself each week.

Being a calm, peaceful parent means taking everyone's needs into account, and respecting each person in the family's needs as valid and important. Being a calm parent does not mean being a martyr and always meeting your family's needs at the expense of your own (and besides, as we've already discussed, sacrificing your needs often ends up affecting everyone negatively in the long term anyway).

No one is going to give you permission to put your own needs first, so consider this your permission slip. As we've already discussed, taking care of yourself and listening to your needs will benefit your whole family, not just you.

Sharing the load

If you live with a partner, one of the best ways to ensure you are getting your needs met is to work towards equally sharing the load of childcare, chores, emotional labour, and 'mental load' (thing like remembering dentist appointments, sending birthday cards, and putting the parent–teacher appointments in the diary) around paid work commitments.

Unlike paid work, much of this work is invisible and not properly valued in our society. (Was there ever a more disparaging phrase than 'She's just a stay-at-home mum'?) The lack of status accorded to this very real work can be read as a sign of how little worth is accorded to taking care of children, something sadly reflected by shockingly low wages for early-years workers and teachers in many parts of the world. Where I live, in the UK, the average nursery worker's salary is less than £9 (around USD$11 or AUD$17) per hour, barely the national living wage.

And it probably won't surprise anyone to read that the

majority of this unpaid work is still being carried out by women, despite more mothers being in the workforce than ever before. And keeping all of these tasks and to-do's in your brain can be exhausting.

I spoke to Jamey Fisher-Perkins, a feminist writer, parenting coach, and mother to two young boys about this:

'Women take on the bulk of tasks in a family related to children and home care, especially the invisible jobs like remembering a complicated schedule, or keeping track of the family's social and community obligations. This happens whether or not mothers are employed in paid work — and, in fact, although you might expect the hours women spend on housework and childcare to be more on parity with their partners if they have paid jobs, the opposite is true. Mothers who have jobs outside the home still do the majority of childcare and housework. They take on about 65 per cent of these responsibilities, whereas their partners do about 35 per cent. The reasons for this are complex and varied, but in the end the breakdown of tasks in a family often comes down to habit, and unspoken patterns from our own childhoods that we fall into in times of stress and exhaustion.'

Jamey continued:

'The simplest way of breaking out of the pattern of mothers bearing too much responsibility while fathers step in to "help" is to speak honestly and clearly about what you see happening in your family. Give language to the patterns you've automatically fallen into without blame — or if you need to blame something, blame the generations of social conditioning that has left men underprepared to step confidently into the role of equal parent and home-maker.

'Make lists together about what needs to be done, and check in regularly about how it feels to take on new responsibilities, or to hand them over. Don't assume that your way is the only way — there are plenty of ways to grow a happy and healthy child. Sharing the load of parenting equally doesn't come naturally to most of us, but it's something worth working towards — for ourselves, and for the next generation of parents that we're raising every day.'

These conversations can be difficult to have, and can be made even harder when juggling childcare and/or home-schooling with one or both parents still working. This framework, based on Nonviolent Communication (which we explored in Chapter One), has helped many of my clients to successfully navigate those discussions:

Explain what the situation is in neutral language: 'I am finding it really hard managing my current workload while taking care of the children all day four days a week.' This is not a time to accuse ('You never help with the kids!') or make generalisations ('You always leave childcare to me!').

Explain how this feels to you: 'I feel worried and stressed and tired.' This shows honesty and vulnerability. Use 'I' statements rather than laying blame, as, if your partner feels attacked, you're more likely to be met with defensiveness than with an open and willing dialogue.

Express your needs: 'I need support and more time to work.' This should be clear, and not a reiteration of your feelings.

Make a request: 'Would you be willing to sit down with me and make a plan for how we can both get our needs met around working time?'

As well as the above, pick a good time to talk. Ideally, when children are not around and when neither of you is busy doing something else. Acknowledge your partner's needs, too, and ask them how they are feeling or what they want, rather than just assuming. Offer to reciprocate and help your partner out, too; kindness is not a limited resource and helping our loved ones makes us feel good.

This framework is, unfortunately, not magic. It won't help if you're in a damaged or abusive relationship, or if your partner refuses to engage. But when you are able to communicate positively and clearly, you leave little room for misunderstanding and increase the likelihood of this request being met with a positive response from your partner.

The marriage meeting

Although it may sound rigid, many relationship experts recommend having a weekly 'marriage meeting' — even if you are not actually married to your partner! As well as being practically helpful, on a deeper level, having regular time set aside to discuss what's going on in your lives can help you both feel secure that you are working together on your relationship.

A typical weekly 30-minute 'meeting' with your partner could be broken down into four parts:

- Expressing appreciation and sharing gratitude for each other. Start by focusing on the positives.
- Running through chores and finances, ensuring that

everything that needs to get done is getting done.

- Scheduling fun activities, including date nights as well as individual and family plans.

- Discussing any problems or challenges that have come up, both in the relationship and in your wider family life. This stops resentments from taking root and clears the air, as well as allowing you both to learn from past hurts and problems.

In this time, you can both review the week that has passed and look forward to the week ahead, discussing any plans in the calendar to ensure you both know what's going on.

You can also schedule in time together every few months to check in more deeply with your wider goals and plans for your family, go over what's been working well recently, review finances and budgets, discuss issues that may have arisen in your marriage or with your children, share hopes and dreams about the future, and set personal, family, and financial goals together.

Self-Care for Ordinary and Extraordinary Times summary

- Your needs deserve to be taken seriously, just as your children's needs do. You deserve time to yourself to pursue your interests and dreams. You are worthy of pleasure, time with those you love, and intellectual stimulation. Your body is deserving of being respected, nourished, and well rested.
- It sounds counterintuitive perhaps, but the best thing you can do during stressful, frightening, or uncertain times is focus on yourself rather than your children. There's a reason we're told to put on our own oxygen masks first, after all.
- Self-care is about finding ways to get your emotional, physical, mental, and intellectual needs met. Self-care will look different to everyone; it should be based on you. Your current unmet needs, your interests, your desires, your hopes and dreams, your personality — all of these will define what good self-care might look like for you.
- Developing compassionate self-regard is a vital act of self-care. Mindfulness can help you to pay attention to how you speak to yourself, and to bring you back into the present.
- If you live with a partner, one of the best ways to ensure you are getting your needs met is to work towards equally sharing the load of childcare, chores, emotional labour and the 'mental load' around paid work commitments.

Afterword

You are enough

Parenting through uncertainty, crisis, and change is so hard.

I know what it's like to have days where just getting out of bed feels like a superhuman feat. Where you feel like your whole brain is taken up with thoughts, worries, lists, and jobs; where you hide in the bathroom, and when little hands bang on the door you cry and cry because you have no space to think.

I know you want the best for your children, but sometimes it feels like you have nothing left to give them.

But I also know this: as a parent, you have already shown yourself to be resilient in the face of enormous change, and capable of tackling the hardest situations. I know that your children are adaptable. They won't hold your bad days against you.

You are already everything your children need, even as you continue to grow alongside them. Right now, just as you are, you are enough.

You are more than enough. You are extraordinary.

References and
further resources

Chapter One

Books

John Bowlby, *A Secure Base*
Lawrence Cohen, *Playful Parenting*
Lawrence Cohen, *The Opposite of Worry*
Teresa Graham Brett, *Parenting for Social Change*
Robin Grille, *Parenting for a Peaceful World*
Janet Lansbury, *No Bad Kids*
Alfie Kohn, *Unconditional Parenting*
Philippa Perry, *The Book You Wish Your Parents Had Read …*
Carl Rogers, *Client Centred Therapy*
Marshall Rosenberg, *Nonviolent Communication*
Daniel Siegel & Mary Hartzell, *Parenting from the Inside Out*
Daniel Siegel & Tina Payne Bryson, *The Whole-Brain Child*

Papers

Avants et al., 'Relation of Childhood Home Environment to Cortical Thickness in Late Adolescence: specificity of experience and timing', 2012

Hirsh-Pasek, Reed & Golinkoff, 'Learning on Hold: cell phones sidetrack parent-child interactions', 2017

Johnston & Davey, 'The Psychological Impact of Negative TV News Bulletins: the catastrophizing of personal worries', 1997

Yu & Smith, 'The Social Origins of Sustained Attention in One Year-Old Human Infants', 2016

Parents and experts quoted

Sal Gould, www.etsy.com/uk/shop/MindfulKin

Lisa Harmer, https://lisa-harmer.com

Carine Robin, https://themontessorifamily.com

Chapter Two

Books

Sharifa Oppenheimer, *Heaven on Earth*

Kim John Payne, *Simplicity Parenting*

Annie Ridout, *The Freelance Mum*

Amanda Blake Soule, *The Rhythm of Family*

Parents and experts quoted

Meagan Wilson, www.meaganrosewilson.com

Claire Chapple, www.instagram.com/educatingella

Gra Conway, www.fredtedandcompany.com

Pippa Hounslow, www.instagram.com/this.mummy.does

Kelly Ellis-Radahd, www.instagram.com/thewaywewaldorf

Lucy Aitkenread, www.lulastic.co.uk

Annie Ridout, www.annieridout.com

Chapter Three

Books

Denaye Barahoma, *Simple Happy Parenting*

Simone Davies, *The Montessori Toddler*

Kim John Payne, *Simplicity Parenting*

Tim Seldin, *How to Raise an Amazing Child the Montessori Way*

Susan Stephenson, *The Joyful Child*

Susan Stephenson, *Child of the World*

Papers

Ginsburg, 'The Importance of Play in Promoting Healthy Child Development and Maintaining Strong Parent-Child Bonds', 2007

Mualem et al., 'The Effect of Movement on Cognitive Performance', 2018

Yogman et al., 'The Power of Play: a pediatric role in enhancing development in young children', 2018

Parents and experts quoted

Hannah Bullivant, www.hannahbullivant.com

Jasmine Chong, www.threeminutemontessori.com

Africa Daley-Clarke, www.instagram.com/thevitamindproject

Bethan Henson, www.somedayslower.com

Dr Leighton Thomas, www.instagram.com/thejonescapades

Chapter Four

Books

Ainsley Arment, *Call of the Wild and Free*

Carol Black, 'Children, Learning, and the "Evaluative Gaze" of School' (an essay that can be found at www.carolblack.org/the-gaze)

Julie Bogart, *The Brave Learner*

Po Bronson & Ashley Merryman, *NurtureShock*

Peter Gray, *Free to Learn*

Megan Cox Gurdon, *The Enchanted Hour*

John Holt, *How Children Learn at Home*

Alfie Kohn, *Punished by Rewards*

Richard Louv, *Last Child in the Woods*

Charlotte Mason, *Home Education*

Barbara Rucci, *Art Workshop for Children*

Alan Thomas and Harriet Pattison, *How Children Learn at Home*

Natalie Wexler, *The Knowledge Gap*

The School of Life, *Big Ideas for Curious Minds*

Papers

America Psychological Association, 'Playtime in Peril', 2009

Australian Council for Educational Research (ACER) and Melbourne University, Social-Emotional Wellbeing (SEW) Survey, 2018

Barnados, 'YouGov Research Survey Reveals Children's Top Back to School Anxieties', 2018

Blackwell et al., 'Implicit Theories of Intelligence Predict Achievement Across an Adolescent Transition: a longitudinal study and an intervention', 2007

Deci et al., 'A meta-analytic review of experiments examining the effects of extrinsic rewards on intrinsic motivation', 1999

Dweck, 'The Perils and Promises of Praise', 2007

Grusec, 'Socializing Concern for Others in the Home', 1991

Henderlong & Lepper, 'The Effects of Praise on Children's Intrinsic Motivation: a review and synthesis', 2002

Institute of European Environmental Policy, 'The Health and Social Benefits of Nature and Biodiversity Protection', 2016

Mueller & Dweck, 'Praise for Intelligence Can Undermine Children's Motivation and Performance', 1998.

Whitbread et al., 'Learning Through Play: a review of the evidence', 2017

University of California, 'Short-term Stress Can Affect Learning and Memory', 2008

Podcasts

Shelf Help: www.thekavanaughreport.com/p/shelf-help-podcast.html
The Montessori Notebook: www.themontessorinotebook.com/the-montessori-notebook-podcast

Videos

Sir Ken Robinson TedX talk: www.ted.com/talks/sir_ken_robinson_do_schools_kill_creativity?

Parents and experts quoted

Leah Boden, www.leahboden.com

Maria Evans, www.mariateencoach.com

Dan Green, www.theweekjunior.co.uk/science-nature

Nicole Kavanaugh, www.thekavanaughreport.com

Ronni Ozpolat, www.multiculturalmotherhood.com

Rachel Stevens, www.littlegulls.com

Chapter Five

Books

Tara Brach, *Radical Compassion*

Susan M. Pollak, *Self-Compassion for Parents*

Thich Nhat Hanh, *Fear*

Alexis Stickland & Beccy Hands, *The Little Book of Self-Care for New Mums*

Parents and experts quoted

Jamey Fisher-Perkins, www.jameyfisherperkins.com

Jodi Garrod, www.instagram.com/mindfulness4mums

Adele Jarrett-Kerr, www.adelejarrettkerr.com

Selected homeschooling books and resources

If you're new to home-based education, pulling together resources can feel daunting and exhausting, and can eat up hours of research time. So, to get you started, here are a few of my favourite materials and online resources. This is by no means an exhaustive list — I've had to restrain myself to a few suggestions per topic area — but I hope it will give you some ideas to explore with your child.

General

If you're looking for some well-designed, solid resources to either teach your child at home from scratch or supplement their school lessons, these are great websites:

- The DK Findout! website is packed full of videos, quizzes, and information on a huge range of subjects: www.dkfindout.com/uk
- The UK BBC bitesize website is absolutely full of resources and ideas for all ages, split into subjects and easy to navigate: www.bbc.co.uk/bitesize
- The US Core Knowledge website is similarly packed full of free ideas and resources for supporting your child's learning at home, and is plotted against grade levels K-6: www.coreknowledge.org
- There is also a UK site tailored to the UK national curriculum for years one to six: www.coreknowledge.org.uk
- If you're in Australia or New Zealand, Cool Australia have lots of materials for kids and educators alike that tie into both the Australian and New Zealand curriculums: www.coolaustralia.org
- For older children, there are thousands of expert-taught courses on Coursera, The Open University, and edX.

Literacy

As I wrote earlier in the book, one of the best things you can do with your children is to read to them, and give them time and space to read too (but don't stop reading to them when they can read themselves). Poetry, non-fiction, comics, jokes, fairy tales, modern fiction, plays — it's all good. Audiobooks, children's podcasts, and authors reading their books online are all good options too.

These websites are packed full of ideas and resources to help your children develop their literacy skills:

- Centre for Literacy in Primary Education: www.clpe.org.uk/clpe/free-resources
- National Literacy Trust: www.literacytrust.org.uk/free-resources
- Royal Shakespeare Company: www.rsc.org.uk/education/teacher-resources
- The Poetry Society: www.resources.poetrysociety.org.uk

Maths

Maths doesn't have to be intimidating or dull, and there are so many fantastic resources available now to really bring it to life.

For pre-schoolers, Numberblocks is a brilliant TV show that introduces simple concepts in an engaging and memorable way. If you have a child aged six or over, they might enjoy learning to code with Scratch: https://scratch.mit.edu. And you can't go wrong with Khan Academy, whatever their age or skill: www.khanacademy.org.

Here are some of our favourite maths books:

- Usborne do a lift-the-flap series of maths books and accompanying activity books that are great for primary/elementary school-age children.
- The Charlesbridge Math Adventures series of picture books bring a range of complex ideas to life for primary/middle school-age children.

- If you're looking for a fun book that covers some complex material as well as going over the basics, *The School of Numbers* by Emily Hawkins is great.
- Whether your child loves maths or not, you can bring the subject to life with biographies of famous mathematicians and thinkers. My daughter has loved reading about Ada Lovelace and Grace Hopper.
- Cooking is also good for introducing practical maths, especially when multiplying or dividing amounts of ingredients. We love *Lunch at 10 Pomegranate Street* by Felicita Sala and DK's *Cooking Step by Step* for younger chefs, and older children and teenagers will be able to use regular recipe books or online recipes.

Science

Don't forget that topics such as space, animal life cycles, dinosaurs, weather, and making slime all come under science. There are many excellent science videos designed for school-age children. Here are some suggestions:

- Mystery Science has lots of great, short videos aimed at children on a huge variety of topics: www.mysteryscience.com.
- The David Attenborough documentaries can be found widely, and make for wonderful nature study and geography lessons. Just check episodes in advance before showing very young or sensitive children, as nature can be brutal at times.
- The Magic School Bus series (older and newer) can be found on Netflix and YouTube and are a really fun way for children to learn about complex scientific ideas.
- The music album *Here Comes Science* by They Might Be Giants deals with lots of different science areas, such as cells and states of matter. They also have albums on numbers and the alphabet. Find them all free on Spotify.

Here are some of our favourite science books:

- *100 Science Experiments*, by Georgina Andrews
- *The Natural History Book*, DK
- *Mr Shaha's Recipes for Wonder*, by Alom Shaha

We also love *The Week: Science and Nature* magazine, and enjoy using science kits.

History

Learning about history is a wonderful way for children to begin to understand the world around them more fully, and it's a subject they tend to be naturally fascinated in. Whether it's making a longboat out of cardboard boxes, making papier-mâché canopic jars, or cooking a Victorian recipe, hands-on activities can add a fun dimension to learning about how people lived long ago.

Here are some ideas for introducing history to your kids:

- The *Horrible Histories* TV series is fun, and can be found on Netflix and iPlayer.
- There are lots of great history documentaries that older children and teens will enjoy watching. I love Mary Beard's work on Rome, but you can find documentaries on any subject. Common Sense Media is a great website to check to see whether something will be suitable for your child's age: www.commonsensemedia. org/lists/best-history-documentaries.
- The DK series *A Child Through Time*, *A Street Through Time*, and *A City Through Time* are all great for bringing different periods of history to life.
- Usborne does a range of fun history books for younger children.
- Older children and teens will enjoy reading historical fiction, or watching films set in different times, and judging how true to real-life events they are.

Art

Just as there's nothing better than letting children get their hands dirty when it comes to practical art, nothing beats seeing artworks in real life. But it's not always possible to do this, so here are some excellent online tours:

- The British Museum: www.britishmuseum.withgoogle.com
- The Louvre: www.louvre.fr/en/visites-en-ligne#tabs
- Monet's house: www.fondation-monet.com/en
- Vatican Museum: www.museivaticani.va/content/museivaticani/en/collezioni/musei/tour-virtuali-elenco.html

There are lots more galleries sharing their collections on Google Arts and Culture. (I recently enjoyed the Van Gogh museum.)

Great books can also bring art to life.

- For younger children, I love the James Mayhew 'Katie' series and the Laurence Anholt 'Anholt's Artists' series.
- For older children, *Vincent's Starry Night and Other Stories: a children's history of art*, by Michael Bird, is excellent.

Music

One of the best ways to bring music to life is to listen to it live. But when you're spending more time than usual at home, that can be tricky. This is where online concerts and clips of music of all styles come into their own. My daughter and I are always finding new music to explore on YouTube, from opera to folk. Here are some wonderful resources to get you started:

- *Peter and the Wolf* is a super introduction to the different instruments of the orchestra. This version is wonderful: www.youtube.com/watch?v=MfM7Y9Pcdzw&t=148s
- *The Carnival of the Animals* is a perfect way to get children moving along to the music, interpreting what they hear.

- The London Philharmonic Orchestra has short videos on YouTube talking about different instruments.
- Children's poet Michael Rosen has a fantastic video with beatbox artist SK Shlomo on beatboxing, which children will find really fun to try: www.youtube.com/watch?v=F3s3FKcLsm8&t=342s
- The Royal Opera House has lots of information on its website: www.roh.org.uk/learning

These books are great for primary/elementary school-age children and come with CDs:

- Genevieve Helsby, *My First Classical Music Book*
- Genevieve Helsby and Karin Eklund, *My First Orchestra Book*
- Robert Levine, *The Story of the Orchestra*

You could ask older children to research classical or folk music that has been sampled in their favourite pop songs. (This happens often.) They may enjoy deepening their understanding of how the music they love was made.

Languages

Languages can be fun to learn alongside your children. You could either expand on a subject they are already familiar with or learn something completely different. There are so many fun resources online for every language you can think of, from music and free audio lessons to printable fact sheets, so you'll be sure to find something your child enjoys. Here are some free resources you might like to begin with:

- Duolingo: www.duolingo.com
- BBC languages website: www.bbc.co.uk/languages
- Beth Manners' CDs on Spotify, for young beginners in French and Spanish.
  For younger learners, buying picture books you're already familiar

with in the language you're looking to learn works well, and you'll find so many simple songs for free online for them to listen to. The Usborne first 1000 words books are great too.

If you have older children or teens learning, they might enjoy comic books, movies, magazines, and pop music in their new language.

Physical activity

Putting on your favourite music for a dance party can be a great way to get everyone moving. Here are some free workouts to keep your children active, no matter the amount of space you have in your home or how much access to the outdoors you have:

- Cosmic Kids yoga: www.cosmickids.com
- Yoga with Adriene: www.yogawithadriene.com/yoga-for-kids
- PE with Joe Wicks: www.thebodycoach.com/blog/pe-with-joe-1254.html

Acknowledgements

They say it takes a village to raise a child. I can tell you that it certainly takes a village to write a book. I would never have written *Extraordinary Parenting* if it hadn't been for my wonderful clients and community, who have been cheering me on since the beginning. Thank you for your suggestions, encouragement, and generosity in sharing so much of yourselves with me.

This project would not have got off the ground in the first place if it wasn't for my excellent agent, Carrie Plitt at Felicity Bryan. Carrie, you brought so much energy and skill to this project, helping me shape and package my idea, and find the right publisher in just four days, something I wouldn't have believed possible. You made the whole process feel far less daunting, and your calm guidance was truly a balm.

It is only because of my ferociously smart and talented editors, Sarah Braybrooke and Molly Slight at Scribe, that this book is in a fit state to be read at all. Thank you for your brilliant ideas, insightful suggestions, and extraordinary attention to detail. Along with Adam Howard, Aoife Datta, Emily Cook, Tace Kelly, and the rest of the Scribe team, you have been a dream team to work with from start to finish.

Thank you for your enthusiasm and commitment to this project, and for pulling off the impossible to bring it to print in such a short space of time.

Writing while juggling my client work and courses would simply not have been possible without my amazing assistant, Sarah Starrs, without whom I doubt I would have been organised enough to write anything at all.

This book has been brought to life with quotes and interviews, and I am so grateful to everyone who took time out of their busy lives to contribute to it. Special mentions are due to Dan Green, Annie Ridout, Carine Robin, and Jodi Garrod — thank you for being so generous with your time and expertise.

Writing during a global health pandemic is not how any author imagines creating their first book, especially when isolated from family and friends. Pippa — thank you for reminding me that I can work under pressure. Elinor, Seb — I'm so grateful to have you to navigate uncertainty with. Kathy, Tom — thanks for all of the playground conversations over coffee. Jamey, Ashleigh, Lisa — you are the best virtual home ed crew I could wish for. Helen, Freyja — thanks for understanding when I repeatedly needed to cancel our plans. Jess — you've got me through more tough patches than you realise. Matilda — thank you for shaping me in so many ways.

To my wonderful parents-in-law, Jill and Dan, thank you for all the Skype read-aloud sessions you did with Frida while I was working, and for all of the support you've given me.

Mamie chèrie, merci pour ton encouragement. Te montrer mes fleurs sur l'internet m'a apporté beaucoup de joie pendant ma période d'écriture. Et mon cher Papi — je pense à toi chaque fois que je plante les petit pois avec Frida.

My sister, Dylan, and brother, Eden — thank you for letting me practice my early parenting skills on you when I was a teenager and you were young children. I got the best of both worlds: the joy of watching you grow up, and your friendship now.

I owe everything I am to my parents, who gave me a truly beautiful childhood. To my dad, James, who is the best storyteller I've ever met: thank you for all those nights on the balcony, and for our conversations on education. And my mum, Agnès, who can bring wonder and delight to the most mundane of moments: thank you for showing me what it means to live with integrity and for teaching me how to mother from the heart.

Darling Sam — thank you for picking up not just the slack, but the whole rope. Writing this book would quite simply have been impossible without you there to step in to homeschool and manage everything singlehandedly while still finding the time to bring me endless cups of tea — which I then let go cold. It is a joy to be married to you, and I'm so glad we are on the same team.

Frida, my love — you are the reason this book exists. Raising and educating you is the greatest honour and delight of my life. Being your mother is better than I could ever have imagined, and I love you with every fibre of my being. Thank you for being you.